The University in Crumbs

The University in Crumbs

A Register of Things Seen and Heard

Robert Porter, Kerry-Ann Porter, and Iain MacKenzie

ROWMAN & LITTLEFIELD
Lanham • Boulder • New York • London

Published by Rowman & Littlefield
An imprint of The Rowman & Littlefield Publishing Group, Inc.
4501 Forbes Boulevard, Suite 200, Lanham, Maryland 20706
www.rowman.com

86-90 Paul Street, London EC2A 4NE

British Library Cataloguing in Publication Information Available

Library of Congress Cataloging-in-Publication Data

Names: Porter, Robert, 1972- author. | Porter, Kerry-Ann, author. | Mackenzie, Iain, 1969– author.
Title: The university in crumbs : a register of things seen and heard / Robert Porter, Kerry-Ann Porter, and Iain MacKenzie.
Description: Lanham, Maryland : Rowman & Littlefield, 2023. | Includes bibliographical references and index. | Summary: "Occupying a space in-between conventional scholarship and imaginative storytelling, The University in Crumbs: A Register of Things Seen and Heard is an experimental work that dramatizes the everyday life of the academy"— Provided by publisher.
Identifiers: LCCN 2023007441 (print) | LCCN 2023007442 (ebook) | ISBN 9781538165324 (cloth) | ISBN 9781538165331 (epub)
Subjects: LCSH: Learning and scholarship—Miscellanea. | College teaching—Miscellanea. | Universities and colleges—Miscellanea.
Classification: LCC AZ106 .P67 2023 (print) | LCC AZ106 (ebook) | DDC 001.2—dc23/eng/20230316
LC record available at https://lccn.loc.gov/2023007441
LC ebook record available at https://lccn.loc.gov/2023007442

'You know that I particularly approve of inventing new words for new ideas. I do not know that the study I call *ideoscopy* can be called a new idea. . . . Ideoscopy consists in describing and classifying the ideas that belong to ordinary experience or that naturally arise in connection with ordinary life, without regard to their being valid or invalid, or to their psychology'.

'We must not begin by talking of pure ideas—vagabond thoughts that tramp the public highways without any human habitation—but must begin with [people] and their conversation'.

—Charles Sanders Peirce

~

Contents

~

Preamble

This is a schematic preamble, not a comprehensive, detailed interpretive framing or introduction. The idea of such an introduction feels a little too strong a responsibility to bear. You see, I am not the author of this text; I have simply helped to pull it together on behalf of its authors: Kerry-Ann, Iain, and Robert. The best I can say here is that I have performed some fairly rudimentary editorial work that will hopefully make the text as user-friendly as possible.

The book you are about to read failed to materialize when it was written, or when the fragments of text that make it up were first put together. It has been some fifteen years or more since Robert, Iain, and Kerry-Ann first started kicking around their idea of doing a book on—what they would often call in more recent conversations with me—'the edu-factory'. In our final conversation before they gave me their blessing to submit the manuscript, I made the point of rather pointedly asking them the question that seemed obvious and pertinent to me only as finishing touches were being put to the text: namely, 'Why were they so reluctant to finish up and prepare the book for publication around the time of its original conception?' I guess that question hadn't occurred to me to ask because I already thought I knew the answer. The answer in my head goes something like this: after the three of them had abandoned the notion of publishing the work anonymously or pseudonymously (around late Summer or early Autumn 2022), they feared that, if published, their candid descriptions of the everyday life of the academy might land them in some hot organizational water; that it could be bad for their careers. There seemed to be a shared feeling among them that they would either publish it in their own name and be damned or abandon the project completely. They seemed to be quite antagonistic to the idea of simultaneously writing candidly and pseudonymously about their experiences of working as academics (a trend that seemed very fashionable in the early 2020s and now seems really rather quaint).[1] As Kerry-Ann, with typical understatement, put it: 'It's a bit hypocritical isn't it!?' Anyway, when I first mooted the idea of finally publishing their reflections on the university back in Winter 2029, they all expressed a desire that it be published in their own names. This process has also been made a bit easier by the fact that in the last few years all of them have retired from academia (Robert being the last to retire, in Spring 2033).

So, given that I thought I already knew the answer, why did I enquire as to why Iain, Kerry-Ann, and Robert had abandoned their proposed project back in the early 2020s? Well, as I read through the fragments of text that are published here for the first time, I began to doubt whether their reluctance to put the work out there in the public domain was simply or exclusively due to fear of landing in hot organizational water. Turns out my hunch was a good one. For each of them, individually, also expressed a specific, if at times rather vague, *intellectual resistance* to the project, if I can put it that way. For example, Kerry-Ann spoke to me about the difficulty of finding the right kind of language to talk about the things she was exercised about at that time, the things that bothered her about university life, and not just in the academy of 2022, but the academy in which she was a young, newly minted lecturer (i.e., the late 1990s). Careful readers will, I think, see some of this difficulty laid out in part 3 below. Iain, for instance, expressed a certain reservation about what he described to me as the rather 'conversational and subjective register' of the book, worrying that, at times, the writing was a little 'too descriptive', not 'rigorous and critical enough'. Robert, too, expressed similar sentiments. Again, careful or attentive readers will see some of these worries play out below in the main body of the text.

In the rest of what remains of this sketchy preamble, I would like to do two things. First, I would like to sketch out the bare structure or outline of the text. Second, I would like to quickly preface the main body of the book by trying to give an initial impression of the kind of feel, texture, or grain of

---

1. For example, edited at the time by Jeff McMahan, Francesca Minerva, and Peter Singer, the first volume of *The Journal of Controversial Ideas* was published in April 2021. This publication prided itself on giving its authors the opportunity to publish pseudonymously. The problem, of course, was that such a journal couldn't work given that the political economy of academic publishing necessitates that individual authorial credit be explicitly given and recognized in a competitive marketplace of ideas where scholars jockey and vie for jobs, grants, promotions, etc. It was a miracle that they managed to get out the five volumes they did.

the work. My hope in doing these two things is that it helps better anchor the reader in the academic lifeworld(s) so vividly portrayed by Kerry-Ann, Robert, and Iain in the pages to come.

A Bare Structure or Outline:
A Series of Five First-Person Reports in
Dialogue with One Another

Stripped back to bare essentials, this work puts a series of five first-person reports in dialogue with one another in an attempt to capture some everyday experiences of academic life, roughly between 2017 and 2022. We shall see that these reports, more often than not, take a dialogical form, registering situated talk or communicative interaction among the authors as a three, as well as their individual exchanges with significant others (e.g., the authors' friends and colleagues).

In part 1, *The 'Other R. D. Laing'*, we actually get all these things together as Iain, Robert, and Kerry-Ann find themselves in a shared conversation with the rather mysterious 'Robert Donald Laing'. Essentially, this is a transcript of a recorded telephone interview that took place in July 2018 (briefly introduced, cleaned up, and edited subsequently by Iain), where all three authors pose questions to Laing, and hear him read some excerpts from the now notorious—some would say scandalous—book: *Stepping into the Breach: Garfinkelian Experiments in the Academic Spectacle*. As you probably already know, 'Laing' is not all that he initially appears to be, and, in the wake of their encounter with him, Kerry-Ann, Robert, and Iain exchange some emails where they begin to reflect on their own emerging project, which they initially frame as a kind of basic or 'banal phenomenology' of their experiences of academic life.

In part 2, *Waiting for Gadu . . .*, Iain tries, in his own way, to make good on this notion of a 'banal phenomenology'. Ostensibly, what Iain provides here is a first-person report, a series of reflections, on a workplace meeting, a meeting to discuss the 'divisional restructuring' that happened at his then academic institution, sometime in 2017. This part of the book stands out from the others as it is pretty much dominated by the author's reflections in monologue form. That is to say, there is little to no dialogue as Iain reflects on his observations; that is, he uses his recorded observations of the events taking place in the meeting room on the day in question (registered in his trusty notebook) to prompt specific reflections and speculations. At one point, drawing on the work of the German sociologist Georg Simmel, Iain refers to his notebook musings as a 'curiously singular and introspective stenography', something that helps him, again riffing on Simmel, to 'catalogue eye gestures' that suggest 'anxiety, suspicion, distrust, and, more generally, antagonism' between the people in the room. A 'banal phenomenology' of eye movements, then, and one that gestures at the shifting social relations set in motion during the rough and tumble of the meeting.

In part 3, Academic World *and the Office Clear-Out*, Kerry-Ann recalls how a clear-out of her academic office in Summer 2020 led to a reconnection with an old friend from her PhD days, a friend she calls 'Mrs Pills'. Finding old copies of *Academic World* at the bottom of a filing cabinet—a Situationist-inspired zine that she and Mrs Pills were both involved in producing during their postgraduate studies in the late 1990s—Kerry-Ann is somewhat disturbed and prompted not only to reflect on the content of the zine, but to think also about the historical and institutional context in which it was produced. After providing the reader with a short introduction to *Academic World*, as well as a few bits of content for illustrative purposes, Kerry-Ann then spends the bulk of this part of the book in a dialogue with her old friend Mrs Pills. What we have reproduced here are specific fragments of some of their online conversations; Zoom recordings, that were subsequently edited by Kerry-Ann in order to iron out some repetition and clean up the talk a little for ease of reading.[2] It is important to say that Mrs Pills (obviously 'Mrs Pills' is a pseudonym) has seen all of the material edited and published here and has given her blessing. The conversational nature of their dialogue; the, at times, earthy tone of their exchanges; and the intimacy of their developing interaction are all thankfully retained in the text as presented.

In part 4, *The Class on 'Space Traders'*, Robert also experiences a disturbance in his academic office, happened upon by his friend and more senior colleague who he finds in a terrible state. 'Professor G', as he pseudonymously calls him, prevails upon Robert for help, advice, or maybe just a kind word, in the aftermath of some negative experiences with a particular group of his students. It would seem that some of Professor G's students have taken exception to the content of his lectures and seminars; they seem to be particularly exercised by his class on Derrick Bell's short story 'Space Traders'. After some initial reflection and discussion of the importance of Derrick Bell's work, Robert then provides a recording of an online dialogue or conversation with Professor G that took place around a week after their initial exchange in his office (i.e., early May 2022). During this period, more broadly (roughly be-

---

2. For all you younger readers and historical amnesiacs, 'Zoom' was a cloud-based video conferencing service that was very popular in the early 2020s, particularly after the first wave of the Covid-19 pandemic hit.

tween Summer 2018 and Spring 2024), both Robert and Professor G would have a regular recorded weekly online meeting or catch-up. In theory, these meetings were about the book project they were working on at the time, but often, Robert tells me, they would veer off in all manner of directions. Unsurprisingly, perhaps, the first meeting after Professor G's 'mini meltdown', as Robert once described it to me, was dominated by a discussion of the former's challenging and antagonistic students. Inspired by reading Kerry-Ann's dialogue with Mrs Pills, Robert similarly set to work editing his conversations with Professor G in a way that tried to capture the vitality and feel of their exchange. As with Mrs Pills, Professor G gave his permission to publish the version you will read here.

The fifth and final part of the book, *The Conference Paper on 'Universities and Critique in a Neoliberal Age'*, begins with Robert, a week on from his 'Space Traders' conversation with Professor G, anticipating the delivery of a paper or 'short provocation' in an upcoming conference. We learn that he is equally attracted and repulsed by the prospect. After sharing his initial feelings about his participation in the 'Universities and Critique in a Neoliberal Age' conference, Robert proceeds to reproduce the detail of the paper, before then providing some rather mordant reflections on how the event unfolded. He particularly zeroes in on an encounter with those who he once described to me as 'the stone-cold ideologues of a shameless culture industry of "critical university studies"'.[3] These mordant reflections are then shared by Robert in an email exchange with Kerry-Ann and Iain in early July 2022. Indeed, it is with this dialogue on email that the text concludes, where we find all three of them again discussing the relative merits (or no) of the proposed project. A project they would then abandon shortly after. Abandon, that is, until now . . .

---

3. It is really irritating that Robert never tells his readers who these 'stone-cold ideologues of a shameless culture industry of critical university studies' are. The best I can do is perhaps interest you in a sampling of some of the supposedly 'critical' takes on the 'neoliberal' university that were out and circulating back when Robert was writing. These include: Lawrence Busch, *Knowledge for Sale: The Neoliberal Takeover of Higher Education* (Cambridge, MA: MIT Press, 2017); John Smyth, *The Toxic University: Zombie Leadership, Academic Rock Stars and Neoliberal Ideology* (London: Palgrave-Macmillan, 2017); Sinead Murphy, *Zombie University: Thinking Under Control* (London: Repeater Books, 2017); Thomas Docherty, *The New Treason of the Intellectuals: Can the University Survive?* (Manchester, Manchester University Press, 2018); Michael Bailey and Des Freedman, eds., *The Assault on Universities: A Manifesto of Resistance* (London: Pluto, 2011); Stefan Collini, *Speaking of Universities* (London: Verso, 2017). Are any of these the 'ideologues' that Robert has in mind? I simply don't know. When I asked him to tell me, his arrogant, smart-ass response was: 'But then you'll only go off and read their books. There's no need for both of us to make that mistake'.

The University in Crumbs:
A Register of Things Seen and Heard

Kerry-Ann came up with the title, *The University in Crumbs: A Register of Things Seen and Heard*, inspired by the very email exchange of July 2022 mentioned a moment ago. Before concluding this preamble, it is perhaps worth saying something more about that as I think it will usefully give the reader an initial impression of the kind of feel, texture, or grain of the work she is about to read. As I'm sure you probably already realize, this is not a traditional academic or scholarly text. It is not a systematic or empirically ambitious project, it makes no claims regarding disinterested, impartial, or objective analysis of the general conditions shaping the organizational life of the university. If the reader is looking for such a general or broad-based analysis, I suggest that she stop reading now and go off in search of those scholars working in the burgeoning field of 'critical university studies', a field of study that has diversified and developed since Robert's diatribe against it in the early 2020s. Though, in fairness to him, this field of study does retain some of the negative characteristics Robert ascribes to it in part 5 below.[4]

Anyway, the more pertinent or pressing point for us is that this book is very much written in a more subjective and conversational register (to steal Iain's phrase from earlier). Further, it is worth noting that the fragments of text presented here, associative as they undoubtedly are, dialogue with one another across any number of *registers*. So, the subtitle of the book, 'a register of things seen and heard', can perhaps take on a few meanings here. Most immediately, of course, is the subjective register of the writing we have been talking about. As emphasized, essentially what is presented in the following pages is a series of five first-person reports, and even though there is a cast of other characters (Laing, Mrs Pills, Professor G, Professor G's 'alt-right' students, the 'critical university studies' crowd . . .) they are always presented from the first-person perspective of either Kerry-Ann, Iain, or Robert. Added to this is a notion of a 'register' in the sociolinguistic sense; the ways we use different words, engage in different styles of communication, in different pragmatic circumstances, to different people, at different times, with different intentions and ends. In this regard, we will see all the authors constantly shifting registers according to the pragmatics of the situation. For

---

4. We should say that in part five we also find Robert praising some scholarly works that he seems happy to shelter under the umbrella of 'critical university studies'. These include: Les Back, *Academic Diary* (London: Goldsmiths Press, 2016); Craig Robertson, *The Filing Cabinet: A Vertical History of Information* (Minneapolis: University of Minnesota Press, 2021); Martin Parker, *Shut Down the Business School* (London: Pluto Press, 2018); Martin Parker, *Against Management; Organization in the Age of Managerialism* (Cambridge: Polity, 2002).

instance, we will find Iain sharing a quiet joke with his colleague 'Chrissy' in a meeting, Kerry-Ann sharing her experiences with 'Mrs Pills' in intimate exasperation and good humour, Robert resentfully baiting and berating the 'critical university studies' crowd at a conference, Iain quoting and interpreting Simmel's 'sociology of the senses', Kerry-Ann parsing the technical language she finds in Wilfred Sellars' *Empiricism and the Philosophy of Mind*, Robert outlining Derrick Bell's 'legal realism' apropos his key concept of 'interest-convergence'. As you will see across all five parts of the text, there is a consistently present and pressing contrast, dialogue even, between a kind of technical academic talk and everyday talk (one minute earthy remarks about Professor G's 'alt-right' students, the next minute reading bits of Roland Barthes' *Mythologies*, one minute a discussion of the 'therapeutic' merits of Richard Rorty's *Philosophy and the Mirror of Nature*, the next palpable frustration and disgust at the everyday sexism in the academy); the repetitious playing of one against the other. Would it be interpretive impertinence on my part to suggest that this shifting of registers is what gives the entire book a kind of consistency, at least in terms of its texture, grain, or feel?

At one point in his discussion of Derrick Bell's 'Space Traders', we find Robert speaking about what he calls 'the gritty, polyvocal vernacular of the language-games specifically chosen to further the story', and I think this is a phrase that we would do well to keep at the forefront of our minds as we go through the book. For even though we are clearly presented, at a schematic or diagrammatic level, with a series of five first-person reports, they will resonate if, and only if, they further a story that, by necessity, speaks to us in tongues, in many voices, through the broader social field in which such reports take on significance to those involved. That social field includes you, dear reader. This might be why some parts of the text may well be easier for you to get your tongue around than others. This is to be expected because polyvocalism, while always more than one voice, is hardly everyone's voice, and never is it the voice from eternity. Let's be clear: speaking in tongues is not a divine experience, but an all too human practice.

I feel I might be getting off track, veering into the kind of introduction or interpretive framing of the text that I precisely said I wouldn't engage in. I am not the author, after all, and this preamble has been preambling, rambling, and rumbling along for perhaps too long already . . .

But one more thing: the 'crumbs'. Kerry-Ann, Robert, and Iain like the idea that they are presenting 'the university' in a rather 'crummy' form. For their rationale, you can look at the email exchange at the end of the book. What I would say, here, by way of concluding this preamble, relates yet again to the register(s) in which the book was written. Put crudely, and as I have already implied, if you are looking for a systematic analysis of the 'university' as a kind of generalized corporate form, if you are looking for a romantic narrative or history of decline in which the very 'idea' of the university has been treasonously betrayed, if you are looking for a political economy and critique of the market forces and consumer logic that shape the academy, if you are looking for a sociologically rich and comprehensive depiction of the possessive individualism that scars contemporary 'academic capitalism', if you are looking for a cross-comparative critique of how various nation-states in the overdeveloped world attempt to audit and control the core business of a university sector that they no longer want to fund from the public purse, or if you are looking for ammunition to politically, or even legally, challenge the classist, gendered, and racialized hierarchies and institutional practices that grease the organizational skids of everyday academic life, then, please, do yourself a favour, and look elsewhere. Look to Robert's frenemies in 'critical university studies'. But, please, I beseech you, be discerning in your tastes, as some of these people really are the disgusting and rather hateful careerist academic capitalists that Robert rather resentfully says they are.

All of this is to say, finally, that you should forget any objectivist pretensions to the last or lasting word on any of the concerns articulated above. For you will need to content yourself with the subjectivist crumbs in this context. But maybe—and as is said in their concluding email exchange—*the crumbs are also the bread* for Kerry-Ann, Iain, and Robert. I do think careful, attentive, open, and generous readers will see in these crumbs something worth seeing. So, please, read on . . .

—David Lewis Moncrieff
14th October
2033

A Note on the In-Text Footnotes

Before you read on, just a quick note on the footnotes in-text. In addition to the preamble above, I am providing some footnotes primarily to reference the scholarly work that Robert, Kerry-Ann, and Iain implicitly and explicitly refer to throughout. Although perhaps less elegant or tidy than endnotes, these in-text footnotes will be useful in that they will also allow us to quickly glance, cross-reference, and move between the text and its contextual backcloth without the need for laboriously flicking back and forth across its pages. They may even aid the reader in foregrounding a little more some of the historical quirks that reflect the time that has lapsed between the crafting of the book in the early 2020s and its publication here and now. I have tried my best to keep speculation or explanation of the contextual backcloth to the book to a minimum. I think, by and large, parts one through to five speak for themselves and you don't need me unnecessarily trifling with your intelligence on that score. That said, there will be moments when I can't resist the temptation.[1]

---

1. For instance, at this moment, I can't resist the temptation of pointing out that at no point do Kerry-Ann, Iain, or Robert express any concern about the carbon footprint of all their online activity. Viewed from our current historical vantage point (late 2033), this seems like a startlingly obvious blind spot. While hardly voluminous, there was, even back in the early 2020s, some scholarly work and political activism pointing directly to the problems associated with the carbon footprint of online life. See, for example, Sven Anderson et al., *States of Entanglement: Data in the Irish Landscape* (Barcelona: Actar Press, 2021).

~

PART ONE

The 'Other R. D. Laing'

Robert Laing seemed to take if not a perverse, then a disturbingly disproportionate, pleasure in introducing himself as the 'other R. D. Laing'. This is how he immediately addressed himself to me when I first approached him as part of our research for this book. *If you'll permit me to introduce myself, Iain: I'm the other R. D. Laing.* Kerry-Ann, Robert, and I were interested in talking to the mysterious Robert Donald Laing for the obvious reason. That is to say, *Stepping into the Breach: Garfinkelian Experiments in the Academic Spectacle* was important to us precisely because we were working on our own book on the contemporary university. Below is an account of our conversation.

Iain MacKenzie (IM). 'Perhaps we could begin with a simple question? Why . . .'

Robert Laing (RDL). 'Sorry to interrupt, but I'm always wary of simple questions, of the very idea that there is anything like a simple question . . .'

IM. 'OK, OK [laughs], well, if not a simple question, then a direct question . . .'

RDL. 'Good, good, I'd prefer those . . .'

IM. 'OK, so what inspired you to write *Stepping into the Breach?*'

RDL. 'Though part of me is loath to admit this in public [laughs], I think it was a sense of righteous indignation, you know what I mean? Didn't Seneca or someone say that anger was the first political emotion? I was angry, angry about the hypocrisy, cowardice, and corruption I found in an institution that I loved, or thought I loved. I know this makes me sound like a bit of a self-righteous prick, but I guess I wanted to expose the academy for the corrupt spectacle it had become, to try to rescue it from the grubby little hands of those who were ruining it. Even as I was writing the book I knew that this motivation was problematic, arrogantly self-indulgent, but as the project continued I went all in and thought, for better or worse, that I had to see it through'.

IM. 'Why did you consider your motivation problematic or arrogantly self-indulgent?'

RDL. 'It was a persistently nagging feeling that I was ill qualified to do the kind of methodological work the project called for. After all, I am a philosopher by trade, rather than a social scientist. In the first instance, I took my cue from a friend, Richard, who happened to mention in passing one day the famous "breaching experiments" of Harold Garfinkel. In the most basic sense, and as everybody knows, Garfinkel's breaching experiments are interesting, funny even, in that they allow us to look at the reactions of social actors in situations where accepted norms, values, or rules are significantly or dramatically violated. I felt, and continue to feel, a bit of impostor syndrome in this context as the work I did never really went beyond rather crudely operationalizing this very basic idea of a breaching experiment. The different examples are not worth rehashing here; they are all in the book [*Stepping into the Breach*] and people can read them for themselves. I can now confess to not really reading enough primary material as I got caught up in the secondary literature on Garfinkel and workplaces; that is, studies of organizations inspired by Garfinkel.[1] So, inspired by such work in the field, I zeroed in on situated action and talk in my own organizational backyard. My aim was one of uncovering the deliberately or intentionally ambiguous and ever-shifting sequencing and ordering of the norms, values, and rules of the corporate entity I wanted to better understand: "the university" that everyone constantly talked about, but always in a curiously abstract or alienating way'.

IM. 'Sorry to cut across, but can I interject here?'

RDL. 'If you like . . . .'

IM. 'What do you mean by the terms "deliberately" and "intentionally" here? Are these terms a little too subjective, especially when you are talking about what is essentially always an emerging and constantly evolving social reality or process? Notions of deliberation and intention seem to presuppose a subject somehow abstracted from the social process, acting on the social world of "the university" from the outside, as it were. No?'

---

1. For a discussion of Garfinkel's influence on workplace studies, see Anne Rawls, 'Harold Garfinkel, Ethnomethodology and Workplace Studies'. *Organization Studies* 29, no.5 (2008): 701–32.

RDL. 'I'm not really sure about that . . . Anyway, what I was interested in, ultimately, I think, was something like the everyday reproduction of a more or less formalized corporate culture or, better still, in understanding the traction that an idea of a cohesive corporate culture—"our university"—gets in the quotidian rough and tumble of organizational life. This is all very abstract at the moment. Let's take a concrete example, from the study'.

Kerry-Ann Porter (KAP). 'Yes, I think that would help . . .'

RDL. 'OK, remember the story about the "Forward Together" meeting, the unveiling of the university-wide strategy document I talk about in the introduction to the book? For, as you know, it was this particular, real-world experience that gave rise to the idea of doing the series of clandestine breaching experiments that make up the main body of the text'.

KAP. 'Yes, of course, when you made that intervention you mean?'

RDL. 'It was an attack . . .'

KAP. [laughs] 'Yes, an attack it certainly was . . .'

RDL. 'Perhaps it would be good to quote the text directly?'

KAP. 'Good idea, Robert!'

RDL. 'OK, let me grab the book and find the relevant passage . . . Right, here goes, this bit starts on page four of my version:

> Every time the senior management team at my university is purged and repopulated with a new bunch of rapacious, ambitious idiots (and this happens more often than you'd think), our new leaders present a new corporate plan, a new strategy bible. This always involves some unveiling ceremony where the new Vice Chancellor attempts to inspire the troops and get them on board with the new programme. I was in a middle management position and therefore had to attend this meeting and then "cascade" the information to the staff that I supposedly had responsibility for. Anyway, as expected, the VC's presentation was the same, banal, repetitive nonsense we had heard from the VC before her and the VC before and the VC before . . .
>
> Just as it was looking like the meeting was coming to an end, though, something interesting happened, something that hadn't, to my knowledge at least, happened before. It is hard to explain or capture the grain and texture of this experience post-hoc and in the abstract, but perhaps an initial way in is to say that the meeting began to take on the kind of audio-visual grammar of a TV game show'.

[RDL breaks character or breaks off from directly quoting the text]

RDL. 'Sorry, that's a bit sloppy and underdeveloped; I should have explained in the book that I was thinking about the philosopher Gilles Deleuze and his well-known essay "Postscript on Societies of Control". As you probably know, Deleuze famously and provocatively suggests that businesses, and various forms of organizational and institutional life more broadly, are more and more resembling TV game shows. As he famously says: "If the stupidest TV game shows are so successful, it's because they're a perfect reflection of the way businesses are run".[2] For my money, this provocation is to be taken very seriously indeed and is a good way of understanding the gamification of the contemporary workplace. You know, when you are in academia, people say things like "watch out for that woman, she's a game player", or "he's completely cynical and will cleverly play any game in town, as long as it advances his career". You've probably heard phrases like that a million times. And I get why people say things like that! But it rests on a problem, a problem that Deleuze, it seems to me anyway, is very alive to. What am I talking about here? Well, these kinds of statements presuppose that there is a relatively unproblematic institutional or corporate game to be played in advance of game time. It presupposes that some "game players" have the savvy, Machiavellian nous or whatever and some don't, or that some are amoral and ambitious enough to play the game, while others can't be arsed or have conscience enough to resist the temptations of the greasy pole. But this is bullshit, I think, or partly bullshit at least. For no-one can know how to play a game in the abstract or in advance without knowing the rules, how the game in question operates in accordance with pre-agreed norms, explicit forms of rule-bound behaviour. I'm here to tell you that's not my experience of academia! For, if we do indeed understand games as implying pre-agreed normative forms of rule-bound behaviour, then comparing the everyday organizational life or the business of a university to a game is misplaced, to say the very least. It is a bit like comparing a fish to a bicycle. So, rather than talk about the cynical, savvy, Machiavellian institutional operator who knows how to "play the game", I think it is better to speak about the broader gamification of the everyday organizational life of the academy, whereby the rules of the game are being continually subject to rapid transformation, and the act of knowing "how to play the game" is always a precarious and risky one, a leap of faith. This is something intuitively understood by Deleuze in his essay on control societies. Anyway, I've rambled long enough, sorry. Let me back to the text . . .'

[RDL picks up the text again . . .]

'Suddenly, rather than drawing to a close, the meeting began to get stretched out by a number of my fellow middle managers who started, in significant

---

2. Gilles Deleuze, 'Postscript on the Societies of Control'. *October* 59 (1992): 4.

numbers, to ask some strangely banal questions of our new VC, questions that were not really questions at all, but statements, grovelling little ass-kissing statements. Statements about the wonderfulness of the new strategy bible (*Moving Forward Together* it was called). Statements to reinforce the greatness, thoughtfulness, and decency of our new VC. Statements that spoke to how the VC's vision of our future corporate culture was finally a vision that they could buy into with all intellectual conscience. As I said, I'd never seen anything like this before at my university. I recalled a conversation with an old friend who often jokingly described his own institution and work life as an "everyday soap opera in the Pol Pot Centre for Change Management". "You know the drill, Robert", Les would often say to me, "A new VC comes in, they clear out the old guard, appoint young, ambitious and stupid lackeys who all go along with the Year Zero strategy, the Pol Pot strategy, of blaming everything bad on the previous regime, while promising the cleanest of clean slates, progress, the whole-hearted assurance that things will get better from here on out . . .".

All of a sudden, boom, I could finally relate to what Les was saying as, one after the other, middle manager 1, middle manager 2, middle manager 3, 4, 5, 6 . . . started in with the Pol Pot inspired slate cleaning. Before I knew what the hell I was doing, I intervened, went on the attack. I was sick of this bullshit and the following words began to trickle, then tumble, then gush, out of my righteously indignant and arrogant mouth. Fuck it I thought, and thought it out loud, then and there, right there in the room. So, I say:

> *I'm sorry, this is fucking ridiculous . . .*
>
> *I mean, what are we doing here? Really? What are we doing? This is supposed to be a meeting about the new university strategy, and we are being told that the aim of the strategy is to enable all of us as staff to participate in a supportive institutional culture that values our work. But all we have witnessed here today is a bunch of ambitious lower and middle-ranking company men and women [I point to a number of colleagues, particularly the ones who asked the ass-kissing questions] auditioning for you [and then I point to the senior management at the top of the room], telling you how great your strategy is. I mean, what the fuck is that?*

Before I could amp up the drama any more, one of the senior executive management team tried to cut me off, employing a gentle comic put-down (but a put-down nonetheless) that aimed to dissipate the tension in the room and get the meeting back on track. This senior manager, Professor X, is a seasoned campaigner, one of the few from the old guard to maintain his status through the recent regime change in the university ("Thank you Dr Laing for your robust intervention, and I confess to often having all sorts of strange thoughts run through my head during meetings such as these. But, best to keep such distracting thoughts to yourself for now, we can discuss them privately offline after the meeting if you still feel the need . . ."). Professor X has a gift for a certain kind of rhetoric, an ability to punctuate his remarks with little comic gestures, an accompanying audio-visual meta-commentary which functions, it seems, to distract and deflate his interlocutor, in this case, me. Whether it is through the exaggeratedly slow raising of his eyebrows and gentle shaking of his head ("Thank you Dr Laing for your robust intervention"), or the well-placed titter or guffaw ("all sorts of strange thoughts run through my head during meetings such as these"), or indeed the gentle, but firm condescension, intersubjectively buttressed by his ability to draw others into his line of vision to reinforce the perceived impetuousness of my outburst ("we can discuss them privately after the meeting if you still feel the need" . . .), the room is left in no doubt about the pragmatic function of his intervention. Professor X titters, he looks at others and they titter! Professor X guffaws, he receives intersubjective reinforcement in the simultaneous guffaws of his colleagues. Professor X raises his eyebrows, shakes his head, and he finds those sitting around him doing the same . . .

What I find in these stylized dramatizations of workplace behaviour (in the learned gutlessness that is choreographed through the gestures of those mimicking their superiors, the fake, shrill, hollow work laugh of company men and women who have laughed that laugh a thousand times and more, laughed the laugh so much that it is now almost an unconscious tic or part of the muscle memory of their face) is the comic itself. In a split second, I remembered those conversations I had with my PhD supervisor about Henri Bergson, my reading of Bergson's famous book *On Laughter*, and particularly Bergson's key idea of the comic as something "mechanical encrusted on the living".[3] Immediately, I imagined my colleagues as marionettes, puppets on a string, in accordance with the comic technology of Bergson's time. But not happy with that thought, my mind wondered further, straying from Bergson and moving toward the 1990 J. G. Ballard novel I was reading at the time, *High Rise*.[4] One of the things I find irritatingly provocative about *High Rise* is the way Ballard describes people in the sparsest of terms, characters seem to lack any psychological depth and are continually defined by their job and the distinction of rank ("a senior academic on the sixth-floor dances with one of the air stewardesses from the second floor"). Then, in that very moment, during this banal spectacle of vacuous, yet predictable, ass-kissing, just when we should all be "Moving Forward

---

3. To understand the nature of the comic, Bergson writes, 'we must go back to the . . . idea . . . of a mechanism superposed upon life. Already, the stiff and starched formality of any ceremonial suggests to us an image of this kind. For as soon as we forget the serious object of a solemnity or a ceremony, those taking part in it give us the impression of puppets in motion. Their mobility seems to adopt as a model the immobility of a formula. It becomes automatism. But complete automatism is only reached in the official, for instance, who performs his duty like a mere machine, or . . . in the unconsciousness that marks an administrative regulation working with inexorable fatality.' Henri Bergson, *Laughter: An Essay on the Meaning of the Comic* (London: Wildside Press, 2008), 45–46.
4. I think this is a hammy in-joke as *High Rise* was published in the 1970s. A point Iain will draw our attention to below. I shall beg your patience till then.

Together", the penny drops for me: the surface-effect of stylized performance masks nothing in particular, nothing deeper in general. The ass-kissers laugh because their boss wants them to laugh! No, they laugh because "the university", whatever it is in that moment, expects their collective participation in some kind of permissible or sanctioned mirth. They laugh in an unselfconsciously non-naturalistic way, because they don't necessarily want to seduce or flatter with delicacy. That takes real work. Realism, even the surface effect of realism, is a real investment of time and effort. No, they simply laugh because it is an easy, ready-to-hand way to preserve the distinction of rank, and their own place in the hierarchy. In these moments, I think to myself, we are less mechanism encrusted on a living organism, as we know Bergson might say, and more the abstract and stylized gesture drained of any embodied vitality or life, a smile without a cat.[5] "Fuck it", I say to myself under my breath. I decide to speak up again, to amp up the drama again:

You may well think this is funny, but I fancy the joke is on you Professor X! Here's what's genuinely funny, tragically funny: I look around this room and I see your colleagues laughing along with you, seemingly enjoying your condescending retort, but they don't give a shit about what you say or think. It is not even so much that they are cynical (though they are!), but that they show no desire to even pretend that you have anything valuable to contribute here. As you were telling me off, I couldn't help but notice that you were constantly looking around for intersubjective reinforcement, and they [I point at a number of people in the room] obliged by laughing when you laughed, raising their eyebrows when you did, shaking their head disapprovingly at your urging. But there was absolutely no life in those gestures! At first it made me think of Henri Bergson's idea of the comic, whereby the mechanical is encrusted onto a living organism. What he has in mind, of course, is the puppet on the string, and I couldn't help but think of what was happening in this meeting as a kind of choreographed puppetry. But it is worse than that, funnier than that, more tragic than that! For they are not even puppets, they are, and you are, mere traces of a stylized gesture, totally lifeless! You should read Ballard! Your future is going to be dreadfully boring. It is as if your face creases, your eyebrows go up and down and your organs oscillate without you even being conscious of it, without you even taking the trouble to feel it. Such lifeless institutionalization would be intolerable to anyone who had the wisdom and desire to see it for what it is. You're all dead, don't you know, you just haven't had the wit to stiffen yet!

I was babbling something rotten by this stage. More significantly, I was genuinely shit scared to hear these words come out of my mouth, but

---

5. This would seem to be a reference to Deleuze's well-known reading of Lewis Carroll's *Alice in Wonderland*. See Gilles Deleuze, *The Logic of Sense* (New York: Columbia University Press, 1990). A reference that is picked up on below by both Robert Laing and Robert Porter.

exhilarated at the same time, an exhilaration which, I realized, was less about some self-righteous indignation or the revolutionary desire to "speak truth to power", and more simply about the crudeness, the literalness, the publicness of my remarks as such. I was buzzing simply because I spoke out, because I acted, I intervened, I attacked. The act of going public, and doing it crudely, seemed to get me going. This was not the crudely literal humour of a Stan Laurel, which is a kind of linguistic working-to-rule (you know, Ollie issues a demand and Stan observes it religiously and literally to the letter, even when the pragmatic circumstances of the utterance actually require its infringement or non-observance). It felt more like a shot at a crude and literal form of inter-subjective comic seduction. Don't be fooled by the haughty intellectualism of my remarks (name-checking Bergson, Ballard, the coded references to Deleuze, purposely delivered over the heads of the audience), for I think what I wanted was actually to seduce my colleagues! Where Professor X garners intersubjec-tive approval from his colleagues through his humorous and rather superior audio-visual meta-commentary on the silliness of my remarks (and let's be honest I was talking silly), I guess I was gambling on engendering intersubjec-tive empathy by attempting as clever and as funny a form of masochistic self-flagellation as I could muster. How could such a thing work? Well, everything rides on the possibility of reading my remarks as a masochistically strident and very public acknowledgment of Professor X's rebuke, but one that has the po-tential to connect to hitherto alienated colleagues, garnering a sympathy that is expressed in a new form of political solidarity (a new "us" against the "senior management"). It was the final line ("You're all dead, don't you know, you just haven't had the wit to stiffen yet . . .") that sent a very small ripple of im-promptu laughter around the room, an involuntary and uncomfortable laugh for some, the kind of laugh perfected in the improvised dramatizations we may well associate with the British filmmaker Mike Leigh; that is, the momentary and unconscious corporeal hijacking of strictly choreographed, domesticated, or otherwise well-behaved bodies.[6] Little bodily explosions do happen when something funny unexpectedly grabs us . . .

To be sure, humour can explode in our faces, and the ecology of emotional and intersubjective relationships it then plays into can change in all sorts of unpredictable ways as a consequence. But perhaps we could retrospectively think about the impromptu ripple of laughter in the "Moving Forward To-gether" meeting as an acceptance, for at least some in the room, of the implicit invitation to join me as fellow, comradely, worker-masochists in this rather painful organizational theatre of the absurd.[7] Perhaps the laughter here is a barely conscious or tacit consent, a barely conscious intersubjective empathy,

---

6. Laing seems to particularly have in mind Leigh's Palme d'Or winning 1996 film *Secrets and Lies*. I say because this particular film is mentioned in a few other places in *Academic Spectacle*.

7. This connecting up of humour, masochism, and work might be seen as another coded reference to Deleuze. See, for example, Gilles Deleuze, *Difference and Repetition* (London: Athlone Press, 1995).

because maybe, just maybe, some colleagues in the room were moved by the anxiety, the anger, the pain, they heard in my voice, and as it reverberated around the room, they maybe began to recognize in it their own anxiety, their own anger, their own pain, their own experience and their own life in the organization. The key here is that the absurdity becomes all too palpable, all too real, all too pressing, something that simply cannot be tolerated any longer precisely because it can no longer be ignored: it is felt empathetically, intersubjectively, maybe even in solidarity . . .'

[RDL breaks character or breaks off from the text]
RDL. 'OK, I'll leave it there . . .'
Robert Porter (RP). 'Thanks for that, really interesting, really funny'.
RDL. 'Thanks, Robert!'
RP. 'I wonder though whether, I mean as you read the text back there, whether you knew what you were doing by adopting this style of writing?'
RDL. 'Style? What do you mean?'
RP 'Well, I suppose I mean you write in a very conversational register, very informal, very funny in parts as I said, while at the same time assuming quite a bit of prior knowledge . . .'
RDL. 'Like what?'
RP. 'Oh, I dunno, say in the passage you read out there. You assume a working knowledge of the contemporary university system, or that your reader is acquainted with Bergson's philosophy of the comic, Deleuze's *Logic of Sense* or whatever . . .'
RDL. 'Again, I acknowledged the sloppiness of not mentioning Deleuze's Postscript . . .'
RP. 'You seem to me to play it almost exclusively for laughs, while simultaneously, or potentially, talking over the heads of your readership. Do you think that is fair?'
RDL. 'If you're suggesting that the work is arrogantly self-indulgent, in a way, then you're accusing me of something I've already admitted to . . .'
RP. 'No! Sorry to cut across you there . . .'
RDL. 'No, go ahead, please . . .'
RP. 'No, I'm thinking of something more than what I think you admitted to above. For, if I've understood you correctly, you seem to be suggesting a kind of arrogance as expressed through a gesture of intellectual or methodological over-reaching, in attempting a form of sociological and empirical research that, strictly speaking, you are not trained for. I get that! But I don't think that's much of an issue. Or, that's not the issue for me . . .'
RDL. 'So what is the issue, Robert?'

RP. 'What I'm trying to suggest to you is that some of the arrogance, self-importance, melodrama that you accuse yourself of in the book—and we can even see it in the bit you just read where you say you are talking "silly", "amping up the drama" etc.—mirrors in some respects the kind of comic seduction that you talk about when recounting the exchange with Professor X et al. Do you see what I mean?'

RDL. 'Perhaps you could put it more directly? As I already said, I don't mind direct questions'.

RP. 'OK, maybe I can put it more bluntly then . . .'

RDL. 'Please try . . .'

RP. 'Well, how to say it . . . OK, let me come back to the idea that you are consciously and quite deliberately engaged in a game of comic seduction, that the comic seductions you detail in the book—like in the example you read just now—are at play across the book as a totality and . . .'

RDL. 'Sorry to interrupt, Robert, but I'm not hearing a question here . . .'

IM. 'What I think Robert is trying to get at, or what his remarks crystallize for me at least, is a problem that Kerry-Ann, Robert, and I all discussed with each other when we first read your book. There was a feeling among us that the book holds in tension two things, two things that sit in an odd, even antagonistic, relationship to one another . . .'

RDL. 'Antagonistic?'

IM. 'Yes, like rival tendencies that bump up against one another, or even undercut one another'.

RDL. 'Sorry, but what tendencies?'

IM. 'Well, and sorry if I'm being obtuse here . . . There is, on the one hand, this constant mockery of organizational or university life, a mockery that is dramatized through the breaching experiments you undertake and then so brilliantly, hilariously, document in the text. But, then, on the other hand, your humour borders on a kind of smugness, haughtiness even, where the narrative that unfolds is one in which you seem to be constantly confronted by idiots—the word "idiot" appears a lot in the text—that are simply begging to be mocked. Risking a generalization about idiots myself, but I would say that experience teaches me that idiots are themselves quick to find idiocy in the world, that they are very quick to hold up a mirror to the idiocies of everyday life, but very rarely do they look for it in the mirror when they get up in the morning. Isn't there a sense that idiocy is often in "the eye of the beholder", to steal a phrase from the philosopher Maxime Rovere, and . . .'

RDL. 'You quoting from pop-philosophy-cum-self-help-books now, Iain?'[8]

IM. [laughs] 'Well, I wouldn't necessarily dismiss Rovere's work as pop philosophy or self-help, BUT, my point in all of this is, I hope, clear enough . . .'

RDL. 'Is it?'

IM. [laughs] 'OK, here's the thing: your smugness undercuts your otherwise funny and engaging critique of the idiocies—and I think we all accept that these idiocies are real and deserve to be exposed—you find in the contemporary academy. Put crudely, nearly everyone we encounter through you is an idiot, and that, to us, seems somewhat narrow, one-sided, not a real reflection of university life as a lived everyday experience. To be sure, there are people who do, and say, idiotic things, but there are also good people, doing the best job they can in often very tricky circumstances. Maybe I could bring in Kerry-Ann and Robert? Is that a fair summation of our initial response to the book? Basically, that the smugness takes the edge off the critique and that an overriding focus on the triumph of the idiots feels a little one-dimensional?'

KAP. 'Yes, I think that's fair . . .'

RP. 'Absolutely!'

RDL. 'Is it my fault that there's an abundance of idiots in academia?'

KAP. [laughs]. 'Well, that seems like a good place to pause and round out this initial part of our discussion'.

RDL. 'Maybe . . . If only to let the thought fester and continue to resonate somewhat before we talk again. Of course, as you say Iain, there are a lot of good people in academia, but they tend not to triumph or have any desire to "seize the means of production in the edu-factory". To quote Rovere back to you Iain, the "idiots always win" . . .'

IM. [laughs] 'Touché, Robert, touché . . .'

KAP. 'Oh, so we see that you're not above reading "pop philosophy" yourself, Dr Laing?'

RDL. [laughs] 'Touché, Kerry-Ann, touché . . .'

Those of you who remember the hullabaloo around the reception of *Stepping into the Breach* will already know that a number of authors (yes authors plural) operated behind the supposedly singular pseudonymous mask of 'Robert Donald Laing'. The interview above was conducted over the phone with one

---

8. The book that Laing is rather arrogantly, I would say idiotically, trying to dismiss as mere pop philosophy or self-help is Maxime Rovere's *How to Deal with Idiots: (And Stop Being One Yourself)* (London: Profile Books, 2021). Oh, the irony . . .

of the authors, perhaps its main author, but she (yes female) and the others involved have subsequently suggested that there were up to twenty-five contributors to the project, a team of people, who performed the various breaching experiments documented in the text. Apparently, or as we have been recently and reliably told, these experiments were performed in universities in Tasmania, Belgium, and Ireland, as well as in the UK. Like everyone else who read the book when it came out, we took it at face value. In *Stepping into the Breach*, 'Laing' does, of course, tells us that he is operating behind a pseudonymous mask and we are often reminded of this by way of a number of hammy in-jokes across the text (for instance, in the excerpt quoted above we find Laing referring explicitly, and rather crudely it has to be said, to J. G. Ballard's *High Rise*).[9] But we assumed the man behind the Ballardian mask was telling us something real about his experiences in, what he called, the 'podunk, duff, regional UK university that I had the misfortune of working in for over eighteen years'. When he said such things we implicitly believed him, and believed him in the same way that we believed he was acting alone. Throughout the book 'Laing' presents as a singular male figure, actually referring to himself at one point as the 'lone gunman taking aim at the superabundant idiocy of everyday university life'. While we obviously recalibrated 'Laing' as female shortly after we gathered to do the telephone interview (though there were a couple of minutes before the interview formally started when Robert and particularly Kerry-Ann seemed unable to quite get their heads around the fact that they were talking to a woman), we initially had no idea that she was one and many, female and male. This we learned in subsequent email exchanges with what we then came to know as 'Laing', the collective assemblage of enunciation, a gaggle or bunch of jokers constantly on the lookout for idiot-academics here, there, and everywhere. We were promised further interviews in various email exchanges, but they never happened, so the pause in the conversation articulated above turned out to be an ongoing pause. We promised that if we published, or made public, any part of our conversation, then we would present it as you have just read it. We kept that promise, after a fashion.

Unlike the dramatics, provocations, and confrontations so characteristic of the Laingian approach adopted in *Stepping into the Breach*, what we hope to do here is something that tends more toward the banal or quotidian, something that is *basically phenomenological*. What could that mean? Or, what will this phenomenology of our lived experiences in the contemporary edu-factory look like in what follows? Let us begin in what might seem a rather

---

9. 'Robert Laing' being the name of one of the central characters in Ballard's story. Hardly subtle . . .

oblique way; that is, by recalling an email exchange between Robert, Kerry-Ann, and I that happened at the very end of August 2018, about a month or so after our telephone conversation with Laing. Again, those familiar with the controversy around the reception of Stepping into the Breach will obviously know that this was only a few days after suspicions first emerged publicly about the authorship and the veracity of the text. Some claimed a participative role in the Laingian collective only to suggest that the 'breaching experiments' they performed were actually just made up, fake, mere figments of an overactive and mischievous imagination. Other parts of the collective assemblage called 'Laing' took issue with this and tried to shore up the authenticity of the project. There were so many arguments, accusations, and counteraccusations, jokes and general pissing-taking going on that we decided to literally pull a bit of an ancient Greek style 'epoche' or 'suspension of judgement' on the whole thing. It wasn't even that there were equally valid reasons for believing A and not-A, it was more a question of an intense buzzing confusion, a kind of sensory overload that initially precipitated in us a form of almost catatonic agnosticism or indifference.

Anyway, below is the email exchange, reproduced here in its rather informal or conversational register. That is to say, the language is a bit rough and ready, the prose rather unpolished, but we have decided to cut and paste the email exchange as it happened; warts and all . . .

From: Robert Porter
Sent: 30 August 2018 09:29
To: Porter, Kerry-Ann; MacKenzie, Iain
Subject: WTF?
Hi guys,
Are you seeing what I'm seeing on social media? Our friend 'Laing' seems to be having something of an 'existential-phenomenological' crisis. The group just seems to be unravelling in public. Do you think this is all part of it? I have to say reading the exchanges there had me reaching for my rather dusty and dog-eared copy of Laing's book The Divided Self. Maybe I'm overanalysing, but some of the phrasing and tone of the exchanges reads like passages from chapter two of Divided Self: 'The existential and phenomenological foundations for the understanding of psychosis'. For example, did you see the whole obscure and obsessively detailed debate and hoo-ha about Freud and Dilthey and who was best at reading 'psycho-social hieroglyphics'? This seems to be a deliberate play on Laing's narrative in chapter two of The Divided Self. Have a look at the second section of the chapter: 'Interpretation

as a function of the relationship with the patient'. I mean, they're taking the piss, aren't they?

Now, I can guess what you both must be thinking. Big deal? So, what? But here's the thing from my perspective, or in terms of our book: aren't we going to be tainted by association if we are seen to be acknowledging our interest in *Stepping into the Breach*? What do you think the publishers and peer-reviewers of the book will think if they see us engaging directly with a project that could be construed, particularly by those who would already be sceptical about the kind of work we do, as the worst kind of 'postmodern' and 'morally vacuous scholarship'? We all know what is behind such fake outrage and choreographed indignation—sure its bullshit, but do we want to give them the rope to hang us with?

Am I being a drama queen here?

R

From: Kerry-Ann Porter
Sent: 30 August 2018 09:33
To: Porter, Robert; MacKenzie, Iain
Subject: RE: WTF?
YES!!!!!

From: Iain MacKenzie
Sent: 30 August 2018 16:43
To: Porter, Kerry-Ann; Porter, Robert
Subject: RE: WTF?
Ha, yes agreed!
Aw'ra,
Iain.

From: Kerry-Ann Porter
Sent: 30 August 2018 22:43
To: Porter, Robert; MacKenzie, Iain
Subject: RE: WTF?
Sorry, just messing about earlier, as I imagine Iain was too . . .

Look, I think we should just have the courage of our convictions here. I think it's OK. Sure, we find interesting ideas and ways of being in the world wherever we find them. We don't have to be 'true' or slavish regarding the source. If I can articulate this as straightforwardly as I can in response to the issues you raise.

The authenticity or veracity of the 'Laing' book is neither here nor there for us. It's got nothing to do with us as we're not drawing directly on the work to make any kind of comparative or empirical claim of our own. As I understand it presently, we are considering putting some of our telephone conversation with 'Laing' in the book. This is not a problem for me as long as we frame it right and stick to the terms we agreed with her about making this exchange public.

So, in this regard, no Robert, we are not going to be tainted by association; assuming, as I said, we get the framing right. Again, if I have understood the conversations about our book correctly, what we want to do is a kind of phenomenology of our experiences in the contemporary academy. A phenomenology that is, as we keep saying to one another, motivated by the possibility of reflecting on the things we confront on a daily basis. Isn't that the project? I know we all felt a little uncomfortable reading *Stepping into the Breach*, thinking that perhaps it was a bit arrogant, haughty, that it enjoyed mocking people in a rather intemperate way. For my money, I think the reason for that, in part, is methodological. It's to do with the way the notion of a 'breaching experiment' was put to work in the text I think. The 'Laing' book seemed to be all about provoking people and then portraying their response to provocation in a negative light. There seemed, to me, to be a kind of score settling, taking the piss out of people they didn't like. I don't think that's what we are interested in. Simply put, what phenomenology gives us is a way to think about how things 'appear', 'manifest', 'present' themselves to us in everyday experience.

As for those who might accuse us of peddling a 'morally vacuous' 'postmodern' cultural studies or whatever way you put it? Who gives a fuck about them? You'll never win them over.

OK, it's getting late and I'm tired. Long story short Robert, chill ☺
Kerry-Ann

From: Iain MacKenzie
Sent: 30 August 2018 23:44
To: Porter, Kerry-Ann; Porter, Robert
Subject: RE: WTF?
Yes, Robert chill out ☺ What KA said . . .
Aw'ra,
Iain.

From: Iain MacKenzie
Sent: 31 August 2018 15:13

To: Porter, Kerry-Ann; Porter, Robert
Subject: RE: WTF?

Just to follow up a bit on what you said KA . . .

If we just try to make as clear as possible our working assumptions. Let's come clean with the reader. We are amateur phenomenologists, at least after a fashion. What does that mean? Well, I think 'phenomenology' is a term that we don't need to be precious about, nor apologize for.

We don't need to be precious about it because we can frame it as a kind of existential preoccupation that our readers can readily tap into. Put simply, as you say KA, phenomenology is an existential preoccupation with what 'appears', what is made 'manifest', what becomes 'present', to us in the day and daily. Simple enough!

We don't need to apologize for the simplicity of this because it will do the work we need it to do. We are not doing textual exegesis of the great philosophers of the modern phenomenological tradition, but are laying out, and trying to make good on, a method of enquiry that will hopefully yield something of interest and import.

OK, a final thought: let's say we are attempting to do a kind of 'banal phenomenology', a bit like the way Billig used to talk about 'banal nationalism'?[10] By which I mean this: let's do some careful and detailed elucidations of experiences we've had, not the piss-taking 'made up' Laing shit (was it made up? . . . Who cares?), but real experiences, that is, experiences we can faithfully describe and bring to life for the reader. Look, I think I can write something here, maybe bringing to life an experience I had a year or so ago—remember me moaning about the 'divisional restructuring'?

Aw'ra,
Iain.

---

10. See Michael Billig, *Banal Nationalism* (London: Sage, 1995).

~

PART TWO

Waiting for Gadu . . .

My friend and colleague 'Chrissy' (not his real name; I sometimes call him that because of a more than passing resemblance to the actor Michael Imperioli, who played the character 'Christopher Moltisanti' in the *The Sopranos*, a character we often see running late for 'business' meetings) was always odds on to make the obvious joke as we waited for the arrival of our new 'Head of Division', Alain Gadu. Chrissy saddled up beside me and whispered ironically, 'Am I early, Estragon?'[1] I shook my head and smiled. 'Sorry Iain', he then said to me; 'nothing you can do about it, that joke was always coming whether you liked it or not . . .'

The reason we were still *waiting for Gadu* to begin and chair this meeting on the much talked about 'divisional restructuring' in our faculty was not clear at this point. The long and detailed email we received about the importance and urgency of the meeting emphasized, more than once, the necessity of a prompt and timely commencement at 2 p.m. Yet, there we were, Chrissy, I, and a number of other colleagues (probably about thirty or forty of us in total) all staring impatiently at our devices, or anxiously off into space. It was close to quarter past the hour before we heard the distinctive, yet muffled, tones of the man of the hour, a noise increasing in volume as he moved down the corridor and ever closer to our room. The noise went up as he and his 'executive assistant' made their way toward us, but their communicative exchange was

---

1. A passing reference to Samuel Beckett's play *Waiting for Godot*, as if you didn't realize.

not oriented to our understanding.[2] Indeed, the two of them, Gadu and his assistant, spent another three or four minutes speaking directly outside the meeting room door (the door had unfortunately been closed by Chrissy on his late/early arrival), and while the noises from the other side of the door variously modulated, their semantic indistinctness remained annoyingly constant. One of our colleagues joked at that moment, something about a kind of 'Charlie Brown wah wah vibe on the other side of the door'. I laughed (she delivered the joke to skilful effect, accompanied by some clown-like gestures that seem to capture the Beckettian atmosphere in the room), but not necessarily in agreement. While seduced somewhat by her humour, the propositional content of the joke, if we can call it that, didn't sit that well with me. For the 'wah wah' of authority figures in Charlie Brown (adults, teachers, etc.) always seemed to signify their lack of significance and necessity. That is to say, authority figures in Charlie Brown play no meaningful role in the drama; they are not needed, except as background noise, quite literally. Now, I guess we could say the same thing about university managers, if we were feeling mischievously resentful enough about it. But perhaps this is the wrong way to go, or, dare to say, not really true enough. Perhaps the crucial difference, the difference that makes a difference, is the absence of indifference among those of us who turned up for the meeting (remember we turned up after all). Charlie and the Peanuts gang always seemed to exhibit a kind of sublime indifference to authority that we could only dream of. We, the rank-and-file university staff, seem too often to obsess about the background noise, forever trying to attune our uncouth and untrained ear to the baroque complications of an institutional or organizational mood music that always seems to border on jarringly discordant. Wasn't it the case that we, the university rank and file, had to always consider ourselves rather excitable and energetic little Kantian bullshit detectors? Indifference to authority? No! Rather, critique of Authority! Indifference to the baroque complications of organizational mood music? Absolutely not! Surely, we want to 'bring our own noise'?! After all, one of my other colleagues in the room, another good friend of mine, had her *Public Enemy* tee shirt on.[3]

Public Enemy tee shirts notwithstanding, Kantian bullshit detection devices notwithstanding, I couldn't help but feel that the management were always more than one step ahead of us when it came to the business of critique. Just as these rather depressing thoughts initially and momentarily flickered through my mind, Alain, our new 'Head of Division', finally appeared: gen-

---

2. This would seem to be a reference to Jürgen Habermas, *The Theory of Communicative Action* (Cambridge: Polity Press, 1986).

3. *Public Enemy* were a New York hip hop band founded in the mid 1980s. 'Bring the Noise' is the second track of their 1988 album *It Takes a Nation of Millions to Hold Us Back*.

tly, almost apologetically, ducking his head through the door, before then settling at the top of a large irregular rectangular(ish) jigsaw of tables that the rest of us were all sat around. For reasons then passing understanding, I decided, at that moment, that I would try to record or register in as much detail as I could the things that were about to happen in the meeting. I'm not usually the kind of person who takes notes at meetings, but I found myself digging into my man bag and pulling out my newly purchased A4 Muji notebook. I then borrowed a decent pen from Chrissy (Chrissy always carried decent pens in his work bag, usually Japanese or Andorran), which he passed to me in mock disgust and with a little whispery question; 'Are you taking the piss, Iain? 'Coz that's a terrible waste of ink!' It was with Chrissy's fancy Andorran pen in hand and his whispery, maybe even caustic, question in my head that the meeting began.

So, what happened in the meeting? Well, and though it undoubtedly may well seem curious or overly intuitive to say so, any perception or recollection I have of what happened seems, in retrospect, to lack a certain distinction, any easily discernible linearity, any straightforwardly chartable timeline of this and then that. When I think back to that afternoon I tend to almost exclusively experience a feeling of being more or less this and then that. I know this sounds all very mysterious and obscure. Perhaps I could describe it in the following way. The memory of the meeting is predominantly associated with an intense feeling of being more and/or less hoodwinked and impotent. This intensity of feeling/being more or less hoodwinked/impotent is connected to a particular self-conception of the kind of academic I am, the particular me that is an academic: namely, the excitable and energetic Kantian bullshit detector mentioned briefly above. This self-conception has its origins in my research work, in particular, a book I wrote in the early 2000s called *The Idea of Pure Critique.*[4] Cutting a long story short, what I wanted to do in that book was to try to enliven and put to work an idea of post-Kantian critique, focusing specifically on the problem of overcoming forms of indifference, apathy, and impotent resignation in contemporary political life. However, my experiences of everyday organizational life in the academy over a number of years have definitely put the thinking expressed in *The Idea of Pure Critique* to the test. The drip, drip, drip effect; the repetition of a slightly worsening difference; the same shit, but slightly worse shittier shit. Indifference, apathy, depressive thoughts have been creeping in, for years now.

Looking back in retrospect, I think this is maybe why I reached for my Muji notebook, why I borrowed Chrissy's pen with the urgency I did, why I

---

4. Iain MacKenzie, *The Idea of Pure Critique* (London: Continuum, 2004).

wrote nearly eight pages of notes in the meeting. Though hardly conscious of it in the moment, I think the notebook represented the promise of active and freely moving thought, a mind, abstracted from depressive ruminations and feelings of impotence. The notebook as an abstract mind, unfolded or extended out from, transcending even, the slumped, contorted and already defeated body I was in possession of that day in the room. The notebook as a faithful register of utterly and irreducibly guttural feelings; intensities in the gut, modulating feelings about being hoodwinked, sharp little reflective flashes of one's own impotence, in particular critical impotence, or, more technically or grandly perhaps, the impotence of critique itself. Yet, at the same time, the notebook is also a sign of manic activity, writing, sparks atop of sparks, a multiplicity of sparks, a sparky comprehension of something brought about through a bringing to light.[5]

It took me quite a while before I began to put Chrissy's pen to work, maybe as much as forty minutes. Perhaps I wasn't sufficiently in the habit of seeing what I was seeing and I needed a bit of time to calibrate. Then, at the top of the first page of my notebook I scribbled two phrases. The first phrase, 'perpetually perishable present', followed below by the second, 'ir-regular jigsaw of mutually antagonistic glances'. I joined the two phrases by drawing curved arrowed lines between them to make them look something like a viciously circular feedback loop, a humorous thought (well, it amused me at any rate) completed, copper-fastened, by the angry, emoji-style face that I sketched in the middle of the loop.

The first phrase was Alain Gadu's. A colleague from the department of philosophy, Alain was, still is, a Bergson scholar and I couldn't help thinking about that when he used the phrase 'perpetually perishable present'. Indeed, I had heard him use that very phrase in a podcast that I had listened to only a couple of weeks earlier. There he used it in a rather technical discussion on Bergson's famous concept of 'duration' and the latter's well-known critique of 'time as space'. He sort-of-botched the phrasing a bit in the meeting, or, more accurately, its use did not quite have the pragmatic force and effect he wanted. Chairing his first meeting as a divisional head, Alain was naturally a bit nervous and eager to please, or, if not please, then certainly eager to get his colleagues on board. As I recall it, the phrase was used at the end of a set of jokey introductory remarks which uncomfortably orbited around what he described as the current 'financial realities facing the newly consti-

---

5. Speculating a little, but Iain's remarks here put me in mind of the kind of phrasing we get in the work of Emanuel Levinas; that is, a notion of 'comprehension' that happens through a form of phenomenological description that is simultaneously 'a bringing to light'. See, for example, Emanuel Levinas, *Totality and Infinity* (Michigan: Duquesne University Press, 1984), 28.

tuted division and the university as a whole'. The 'perpetually perishable present' remark was a mock sociological gesture that meant to signify that Alain understood his colleague's anxieties in the current tricky financial climate. He knew, and was honest enough to say this at the beginning of the meeting, that for the previous couple of weeks rumours had been swirling around that the 'divisional restructuring' he was charged with leading was nothing more than thinly veiled cover for job cuts. Credit where it's due, he did not waste much time in confirming the rumours. The basic message was simple. The staff budget, 'our most precious and costly resource' as he ironically put, was too high and the wage bill for the new division had to come down by about 20 per cent. This stab in the dark at irony seemed to have the opposite effect to the one he intended. The ironic quote ('our most precious and costly resource') came from the mouth of a senior-management draft consultation document on a proposed 'Voluntary Severance Scheme' (VSS) he was in the process of handing out to everyone in that very moment he uttered the phrase. I genuinely believe this was an attempt at empathy and humour, a kind of comedic ventriloquism, but, honestly, what an idiotic thing for him to say? It immediately confirmed in my mind that he was very ill suited to the role of divisional head: a position he was convinced, against his own better judgment I think, to take on. As Alain often used to say, again following Bergson, a good concept is like a finely cut and well-fitted suit. On my Muji notebook, I scribbled: 'Mr Gadu or Mr Byrne'.[6] Then, I further amused myself at his expense with my own rather unfunnily botched Bergsonian phrase: 'Alain the mechanical manager puppet encrusted on the living Alain'.[7] I showed my scribbles to Chrissy sat beside me. He half smiled and half grimaced at me, inducing a bit of guilt on my part as I felt bad about taking the piss out of Alain. Yes, there was an organizational or structural idiocy to proceedings, but it was too easy to dismiss Alain as an idiot or, worse still, as an unfeeling, mechanical, slasher puppet for senior management.

It was at this point that my gut started playing up, but I flattered myself that my belly was moved in empathy as well as in self-interest. I felt for Alain. I knew he was going to kop a lot of abuse from the room he had singularly failed to read in the first instance. I knew Alain was playing with knives, that his stab at empathetic humour would fail to cut through the moment copies of the draft VSS document found their way into the hands

---

6. I'm guessing this is a reference to the lead singer of the 1980s band *Talking Heads* as he (Mr David Byrne) was known for wearing rather oversized suits. Hilarious . . .

7. An obvious reference to Henri Bergson, *Laughter: An Essay on the Meaning of the Comic* (London: Wildside Press, 2008).

of his soon-to-be righteously indignant colleagues. Predictably enough, this body of critically trained pedants and textualists carved him up good and proper by carving up the document he gave them. Strict adherence to the text automatically exposes ambiguity and, one by one, colleagues developed their own, often highly individualized, ethical critique of the text. Like de Beauvoir disciples fighting over a meaning against the existential absurdities of the text, they picked apart the document line by line.[8] The specific details of the increasingly heated dialogical to and fro are perhaps less important than the mannerist fashion in which it was progressively conducted. By this I mean that the discussions in the meeting began to draw out, or draw attention to, the stylistics and affectations that so often remain hidden in plain sight in discursive performance. I distinctly remember the jabbing effect of the specific questions being asked at the beginning of the meeting giving way to a numbing, almost meditative, repetitiousness. The same type of question ('What do you or the senior management mean in this bit of the document when you say . . . ?') impatiently, simultaneously, buttressed by the same type of subtextual rhetorical reveal ('Of course, what the document really means . . . ') on repeat; a mantra of righteous indignation slowly but surely being emptied out of meaning, pragmatic force, and effect.

At that point, any pretence of a genuine communicative exchange oriented to mutual understanding just ebbed away. To be sure, sparks were really flying, but they were gestural, stylistic, mannerist sparks that called attention not simply to some external world being represented ('The senior management are . . .'), but, more significantly, to an internal world, a kind of introspective reflection, but pushed outward by way of a particular gestural economy ('Don't you realize the damage, anxiety, stress you are causing in me . . .'). This brings us me to the second phrase or thought captured above in the Muji: namely, the gestural economy that is the 'irregular jigsaw of mutually antagonistic glances'. This notion morphed during the meeting and became a rough and ready heuristic for how I would read what was happening in the room on that day, as well as how I would go on to think about what was documented in the notebook in the days to come. I recalled thinking, then recording in the Muji, 'Simmel?—didn't he say something about the glance or the eye?' 'Is that where this phrase or thought about antagonistic glances came from?' 'Didn't I read something about that in that Ervin Goffman book I was looking at the other day?' For once, my memory held good. For a couple of days after the meeting I reread my Simmel remark in the notebook, realizing I was right when I managed to dig out a quote from Sim-

---

8. The off-hand, even licentious, reference here is to Simone de Beauvoir, *The Ethics of Ambiguity* (New York: Philosophical Library, 1948).

mel's piece on the 'sociology of the senses', courtesy of 'that Ervin Goffman book'; namely, *Behaviour in Public Places*. It is worth quoting this in a bit of detail. Simmel writes:

> Of the special sense organs, the eye has a uniquely sociological function. The union and interaction of individuals is based upon mutual glances. This is perhaps the most direct and purest reciprocity that exists. The highest psychic reaction, however, in which the glances of eye to eye unite men, crystallizes into no objective structure; the unity which arises . . . is present in the occasion and is dissolved in the function . . . No objective trace of this relationship is left behind . . . The interaction of eye to eye dies in the moment in which the directness of the function is lost. But the totality of social relations of human beings, their self-assertion and self-abnegation, their intimacies and estrangements, would be changed in unpredictable ways if there occurred no glance of eye to eye. The mutual glance between persons, in distinction from the simple sight or observation of the other, signified a wholly . . . unique union between them.[9]

In my notebook, I instinctively started to catalogue gestures, mostly eye gestures, and mostly glances that tended to suggest anxiety, suspicion, distrust, and, more generally, antagonism. Without consciously thinking about it too much at the time (though Simmel's 'sociology of the senses' was already clearly playing on my mind here), I started to engage in a curiously singular and introspective stenography, one developed on the hoof and out of necessity; a little abbreviated symbolic writing system that was needed to keep pace with what was happening in the room. When cataloguing the glances of colleagues who I knew by name I provided an initial or two, when I couldn't remember names, or didn't know the person in question, I used 'AN Other' at the beginning, before further shortening it to 'AN'. All very cryptic, I know, so let's try an example.

'AG keeps nervously glancing sideways to C and AN while being grilled by PS on what 'voluntary' means . . .'

Initially, it might be useful to simply register the connections specifically between 'AG' (Alain Gadu), 'PS' (Prue Seaman, one of our colleagues from the law school and staunch trade unionist), and 'C' (my buddy Chrissy, not only a good friend of mine, but a close buddy of Prue's). I just can't remember who 'AN' is here, though I fancy it might be an anthropologist friend of Prue's. Anyway, Prue and Chrissy have extensive experience in the local trade union branch, particularly in various forms of 'case-work' where they

---

9. Simmel, cited in Ervin Goffman, *Behaviour in Public Places* (New York: The Free Press, 1963), 93.

would represent union colleagues in disputes with management. Prue, the senior of the two in rank and age, has particular first-hand experience in representing colleagues through previous rounds of jobs cuts in years gone by. Unsurprisingly, she wastes no time in prefacing her particularly pointed questions for Alain by sharing the hard-earned wisdom of those past experiences with the whole room. She explains that, in her experience, many a supposedly 'voluntary' severance scheme ends up being anything but 'voluntary', that we should be very suspicious and distrustful of management tactics as they have a past track record in 'forcing colleagues to go *voluntarily*'. As we might expect from a legal scholar, she speaks with economy, clarity, and precision, detailing example upon example, instance upon instance, piling up evidence to substantiate the reasonableness of her deep suspicion and distrust of management. Though it might seem rather odd to say this of a colleague who is so articulate and razor sharp in her verbal argumentation, but what initially seemed to carry the real pragmatic force and effect in the room was the rapidity of her eye movement, her optical agility, endurance, and egalitarian openness. The interactional union of mutual glances talked about by Simmel is operationalized in a very direct and effective way by Prue, a product of both her legal training and union experience no doubt. She immediately has an eye for the collective, the gesture of solidarity. I quickly registered this gestural movement of the eye in the notebook. The following is a faithful reproduction:

PRUE'S EITHER/OR[10]

EITHER

a) 'P mouths or ventriloquizes management discourse in the VS document with a rolling glance upwards and sideways and always in the direction of AG'.

OR

b) 'When detailing previous historical examples of challenging the "sly and cunning tactics" used by management in "forcing colleague's voluntary retirement", P obsessively and repetitiously punctuates her remarks by constantly shifting her glance, from eye to eye, to every eye in the room she can connect with'.

It is as if the noting of these actions in the Muji simultaneously allows me to singularly lock my gaze on Prue, almost to the exclusion of all else. All I see in these moments are these particular movements of the eye that happen again and again and as I focus ever more closely on the eyes it becomes more

---

10. It would seem that Iain has Kierkegaard on his mind in this context. Indeed, we shall see that Iain, Kerry-Ann, and Robert will all talk about the great man at the end of part 5. The text being implicitly referred to here is, of course, Søren Kierkegaard, *Either/Or: A Crumb of Life* (London: Penguin, 2004).

and more clear that her discourse is almost entirely animated by the two gestures registered in the notebook. Through EITHER a) we get the ironic or comedic ventriloquism that Prue latches onto and turns against Alain as the representative of 'management' in the room. The aim here, I think, is almost to bracket out everything in the VSS document, put it out of play as it were, alienate the words from any context in which they could be made to make sense, to nakedly reveal them in all their instrumental, economic, and political contingency.[11] Through OR b) we see the attempt at empathy, particularly off the back of Alain's singular failure to show any. Here the desire is to see eye to eye with a deadly earnestness. No heavy-handed or awkward jokes, just gestures of solemn solidarity, a desire to delineate the shape and form of the struggles to come with management. An insistent play of the eye that tries to ensure that Prue and her union colleagues are not only prepared to fight the good fight on their colleague's behalf, but, and perhaps more importantly, that history shows that they know how to fight this fight, that they are battle-hardened and not simply war-weary.

Underneath the EITHER/OR of a) and b) documented above, I then decided to recalibrate or reshape them by setting them side by side in the notebook like so:

EITHER/OR	
a) 'P mouths or ventriloquizes management discourse in the VS document with a rolling glance upwards and sideways and always in the direction of AG.'	b) When detailing previous historical examples of challenging the 'sly and cunning tactics' used by management in 'forcing colleagues' voluntary retirement', P obsessively and repetitiously punctuates her remarks by constantly shifting her glance, from eye to eye, to every eye in the room she can connect with.
SC - *****	SC - **
SAD - *************	SAD - *******************
'SAD' GRINDS THE GEARS OF MUTUAL ANTAGONISM	

Drawing a central line through and bisecting a) and b) above, almost in the style of rudimentary accountant's ledger, and unlocking my gaze on Prue,

11. Attentive or philosophically informed readers may note that the language used by Iain here has a distinct phenomenological flavour to it. For instance, phrases like 'bracket out' and 'put it out of play' bring to mind the notion of 'epoche', not in the ancient Greek sense that is talked about in part 1, but in the more modern Husserlian sense. See Edmund Husserl, *Logical Investigations* (London: Routledge, 1973); Edmund Husserl, *The Crisis of European Sciences* (Evanston, IL: Northwestern University Press, 1970).

I then proceed to attempt to code the movements of the eye around the rest of the room.

Under the first, left of centre, entry—namely a) 'P mouths or ventrilo-quizes management discourse in the VS document with a rolling glance upwards and sideways and always in the direction of AG'—I try to gauge how various colleagues in the room, or at least those in my line of vision, respond to Prue's continual playing out of this distinctively mannerist refrain. Where I detect a sympathetic eye or emanations of solidarity and comradeship, I code it 'SC', numbering the instances accordingly with ****. Where I detect a sceptical eye, apathy, or atomistic drift I code it 'SAD', numbering in the same way with ****. As you can see from the detail in the Muji reproduced above, I am clearly sensing more scepticism than solidarity.

Under the second, right of centre, entry—namely b) 'When detailing pre-vious historical examples of challenging the "sly and cunning tactics" used by management in "forcing colleague's voluntary retirement", P obsessively and repetitiously punctuates her remarks by constantly shift her glance, from eye to eye, to every eye in the room she can connect with'—I repeat the same codes: 'SC' for solidarity and comradeship and 'SAD' for scepticism, apathy, and atomistic drift. Again, the scepticism seems ever stronger and the soli-darity shown seems pretty minimal indeed .

The results registered in the notebook make for 'SAD' reading, at least from Prue's union perspective, and mine too, I have to admit. Perhaps this is what I was already vaguely gesturing at with the phrasing—of 'mutually antagonistic glances'—I used at the beginning of the meeting? Perhaps the angry emoji face I drew to amuse myself always-already spoke to an unac-knowledged concern and doubt I had about the possibility of developing any kind of solidarity in the room? Further, as you can see from fragments of the Muji text reproduced above, it also seems to me that the scepticism, apathy, atomism, and drift shown by colleagues that day were like the gears that grind and get the mutual antagonism going. 'SAD' GRINDS THE GEARS OF MUTUAL ANTAGONISM. What does that mean exactly?

Well, what I hope is beginning to become clear is that this mutual antago-nism was never simply or exclusively between some representative of man-agement (Alain as the new divisional head) as against the represented work-ers (Prue and the local union branch she spoke in the name of), somehow refined and sharpened in the cut and thrust of a spikey dialogical exchange that positioned them in an ever more purified, ideologically entrenched, op-position. No, not a bit of it. Of course, particularly early on, there were ele-ments of this, moments in which it felt like a more traditional spat between 'the management' and 'the workers'. However, as the meeting progressed the antagonism became less and less ideologically defined, less sharp, more diffuse, blended into a soup of individualistic academic atomism, practiced by a classless class of people motivated by an ethic or image of their own 'authenticity', where 'authenticity' brings to mind Charles Taylor's famous critique of a kind of self-absorption, the obsessive desire for 'my' self-fulfilment or self-actualization, the 'me' floating in abstraction from the common ties and values that should be binding us together.[12]

Whenever I read and reread the eight pages of notes from that day, the same impression of an irregularly 'SAD' jigsaw of mutual antagonism seems to emerge and then inevitably fall into place. The angry emoji face seems ever more prescient to me at this retrospective point, and if it retains an element of the comic, it is clearly tragi-comic. The oppositional stance, the becoming antagonistic toward something, almost immediately and tragically becomes diluted, diffuse, and hollowed out by the criss-crossing mutual antagonism colleagues showed for one another. Time and again we find that 'being in opposition' or 'being against' peters out into a rather ridiculous, even comic, 'being for me', 'what about me?', 'you don't know what it feels like to be me!'.

I'd like to conclude with a few quick reflections or lines of thought that have remained with me since that day when we met with my friend, the then newly minted divisional head Alain Gadu. These reflections I will register and catalogue in a three, as you see below. Even though these thoughts are very much coloured by the particular context of our meeting, I do wonder if we could think of them as gesturing toward a more general taxonomic picture that could emerge if we join the dots of variously documented glances, not just in the specific exchanges I have been talking about here, but perhaps in other encounters elsewhere in the contemporary 'edu-factory', or, more broadly still, in other forms of organizational or work life? Could we even think of these reflections and thoughts as just a few of the many possible lines that could potentially get continually drawn around our collectively 'SAD' eyes?

1. The glance that draws a line from the worker protagonist to the management antagonist is unmistakably present, particularly at the beginning of the meeting. But it is perhaps best classified as a Simmel glance, momentary, fleeting, signifying a unitary moment that immediately dissolves in its function. The glance never seems to harden, endure in a longer look, let alone a considered stare of any duration whatever. The optical cable or eye line from worker to management is cut

---

12. See Charles Taylor, *The Ethics of Authenticity* (Cambridge, MA: Harvard University Press, 1991).

in fear or, what amounts to the same thing, in the worker's fearful hope against all hope that the axe will fall on another if 'I' refrain from staring down the manager-antagonist. The downcast eye, while not the eye of the tiger, is perhaps the eye of the survivor, for now, this time, perhaps . . .

2. The glances bundling up only then to split apart as they criss-cross from worker to worker, the endless swapping of the protagonist and antagonist persona, the internalization and externalization of the management gaze. Think of a bundled ball of elastic bands, fraying and unravelling due to the radiation, the toxicity, heat, and stress of a hostile environment. The usual or familiar story of workers turning on one another, blaming one another, a depressingly resonant experience for those of us who work in the edu-factory of 'scarce resources'. With apologies again to Simmel, the function here tends to be one of blame and suspicion. The glance communicating a sense of injustice, that it is partly your fault that we are in this mess. The media studies lecturer running the most popular courses in the division glances with incredulity at the privileged complaining of the research professor in philosophy who, we suspect, doesn't even bother teaching the few students that he and his fellow philosophers have managed to recruit this academic year. Turn and turn-about, we turn our suspicions on the Kantian bullshit detectors by calling bullshit on them.

3. This is a sight for sore management eyes as the internalization of the ideology of 'scarce resources' continues to effectively play out among increasingly antagonistic and atomized staff. In this regard, Alain, the eyes of management in this context, can begin to find his sea legs, or get into his street stride. Glancing across eye to eye of antagonistic workers provides clues as to where the divisional fault lines lie, and where these might be exploited. The old divide-and-conquer trick. Simmel on speed, dissolve as a kind of accelerated function, time and again, the worker-to-worker glances of blame and suspicion unwittingly revealing what was hitherto introspective, intimate, the still unspoken visible politics of 'scarce resources' now externalized, on show, for all to see. No words needed! The management glance is in a class of its own: motivated by the promise of a complete dissolve, of any comradely dialogue dying an almost immediate death in this or that interactional moment. What remains after this relativized death? Well, the promise and fantasy of the eternal life of a management gaze that endures, the all-seeing eye that never stops seeing the fault lines to exploit.

~

PART THREE

Academic World and the Office Clear-Out

I formally entered the academic world as a university lecturer in late 1999. I was recently reminded of a conversation I had on my first day on the job with a then-senior colleague who popped her head around the slightly ajar door of my new office and introduced herself with the following questions and answers: 'I take it you are the new girl? Kerry-Ann, isn't it? Your office is looking a little sparse there, no? Can I give you a friendly bit of advice? Try to keep it that way. Try to clear your office out every so often. I'm retiring in six months' time and I can't tell you the amount of stuff I'm going to have to wade through'.

I was reminded of that conversation, naturally enough, when I found myself in exactly the same predicament. I wasn't retiring as such, but moving to a new campus building, a new work environment, to be honest, a place that looked like a dreary call centre. Anyway, I had to downsize, which is why the office clear-out needed to be as brutally unsentimental as I could manage. This was always going to be tricky, as I am a bit of a hoarder, sentimentally so, brutally so. For me the process of clearing out is difficult because one is immediately surrounded by so much stuff that seduces, detains, throws you off-track, or back on yourself. I once heard a friend (and fellow hoarder) describe this experience as a kind of 'sentimental re-education'. I was never quite sure what he meant by that, but I sort of vaguely understood the phrase to involve a form of irreducibly immersive empathy garnered through the encounter with something *other in the present*. Whether it was getting rid of old photographs that I had already scanned and saved on my laptop; baby clothes, once worn by our now two late-teenage girls, supposedly destined for the charity shop; or birthday cards and other ephemera from friends and family, my response to this *otherness in the present* was always the same. I would stop dead in my tracks, become immobilized by way of journeying back, never making any real headway with the clear-out. I would surround myself with the stuff, go on my journey with it, sentimentally re-educate myself about things forgotten, times gone by, then carefully put it back in the place it had been previously stored.

This was not an option here though. I was moving from a rather large office with around twenty years of stuff (a room I spent most of my working week in) to a shared, open office that I had very little intention of spending any time in. Something had to give. So, I cleared a week in my Summer diary and, by and large, knuckled down to it, filling bag after bag with what I'd tried to convince myself were copious amounts of meaningless crap. I was doing really well until about three days in, when at the bottom of my filing cabinet I found a bunch of old copies of a magazine that I coproduced with a group of friends during our time as PhD students together (1995 to 1998). Inspired at the time by the Situationist zine *Processed World*, we produced around ten or eleven issues of our very own publication: namely, *Academic World*. For those of you unfamiliar with the magazine *Processed World*, you can do what I militantly prohibit my own students from ever doing; that is, Google it and look it up on Wikipedia. If you do, you will find the following description:

> *Processed World* is an anti-capitalist, anti-authoritarian magazine focused on the oppressions and absurdities of office work, which, at the time the magazine began, was becoming automated. The magazine was founded by Chris Carlsson, Caitlin Manning, and Adam Cornford in 1981. No new issues have been produced since 2005.[1]

Better still, this Wikipedia entry directs you to another site, which is nothing less than a full archive of back issues of *Processed World*. Here we find a much more detailed description, some of which is quoted here:

> *Processed World* magazine was founded in 1981 by a small group of dissidents, mostly in their twenties, who were then working in San Francisco's financial district. The magazine's creators found themselves using their only marketable skill after years of university education: 'handling information.' In spite of being employed in offices as 'temps,' few really thought of themselves as 'office

---

1. The link is dead now, but Kerry-Ann included it in her original draft of this part of the book and I include it here: https://en.wikipedia.org/wiki/Processed_World.

workers.' More common was the hopeful assertion that they were photographers, writers, artists, dancers, historians, or philosophers.

Beyond these creative ambitions, the choice to work 'temp' was also a refusal to join the rush toward business/yuppie professionalism. Instead of 40–70 hour weeks of thankless corporate career climbing, they sought more free time to pursue their creative instincts . . . Thus, from the start, the project's expressed purpose was twofold: to serve as a contact point and forum for malcontent office workers (and wage-workers in general) and to provide a creative outlet for people whose talents were blocked by what they were doing for money . . .

From its inception *Processed World* has sought to end the silence surrounding the underside of the Information Age. The participant's political background and detailed outlook continues to be varied, a non-doctrinaire hybrid of traditions and theories. They have in common being against capital and wage labour, nationalism and governments, and for the free association of human beings in collectively determining and satisfying their needs and desires . . .

By serving as a forum for 'ordinary' workers, *Processed World* has reinforced the, often suppressed, truth that social knowledge and subversive wisdom flow from people's daily lives and not from an ideology or group of experts. By building a radical publication around art and humour, *Processed World* has reemphasized the importance of immediate enjoyment, both for surviving this insane world, and for reintroducing fun into radical attempts to change it.[2]

We slavishly modelled our very own *Academic World* on *Processed World*. We tried to have the same mix of material: bits of writing; comic book humour; silly, make-believe ads; fake letters to the editor.[3] I suppose the content that was most grounded in the reality of our daily experience was the thing that probably looked the most abstract and weird from the outside. 'The secret diary of Professor C Wright Pills, aged 44¼, was weird, very weird, the particular preoccupation of one member of our group, but a preoccupation that spoke to us all. I don't want to reveal her real identity, so we shall call her by the pen name she adopted in the magazine, 'Mrs Professor C Wright Pills'. Mrs Pills, unlike the rest of *Academic World* collective, didn't really involve herself too much in the nitty gritty of running the magazine, or in the logistics of pulling the content together. While the rest of us pitched in designing the fake ads, writing the make-believe letters to the editors, sketching the

---

2. The following link remains live: https://archive.org/details/processedworld.
3. For a really concrete sense of the look and feel of the magazine, see Chris Carlson and Mark Leger, eds., *Bad Attitude: The Processed World Anthology* (London: Verso, 1990). While hardly voluminous, there is some scholarly work that engages interestingly with the *Processed World* project. See, for instance, Steven Wright, 'Beyond a Bad Attitude? Information Workers and Their Prospects through the Pages of *Processed World*', *Journal of Information Ethics* 20, no. 2 (2011): 1–25. Also, have a look at Gavin Mueller, *Breaking Things at Work: The Luddites Were Right About Why You Hate Your Job* (London: Verso, 2021), 101–4.

comic strips, etc., Mrs Pills tended to keep her distance. But, she was never late, not once, when it came to submitting the various diary entries that appear across all but one or two of the issues we put out. In fact, in some of the issues (for example, the 'Sex' issue, or the issue on 'Filing Cabinets') Mrs Pills provided more than one of her husband's diary entries. Some context is needed here: the basic conceit was that Mrs Pills would sneak a quick peek at her husband's diary before bed and take a Polaroid of it, obviously without his knowledge. So, the diary entries always appeared as a series of Polaroid snaps—though we should say that this was not very well thought or designed out as the Polaroid frame was simply sketched with a pencil and the text was then roughly handwritten in the same. All very messy, but we prided ourselves on our punkish DIY, devil-may-care attitude. Besides all that, what was really interesting about this content was its, let's call it, 'intellectual conceit'. For Professor C Wright Pills was a 'therapist for concepts', not a therapist of concepts (some latter-day Ronnie Laing) but, to repeat, a *therapist for concepts*. Here's a quick glimpse of some of the text from that 'Sex' issue I mentioned a moment ago. This will hopefully show you what I mean by the idea of a *therapy for concepts*:

Monday 7th July 1997—Truth with a capital T, yet again . . .

My regular weekly 2pm appointment with Truth with a capital T is really starting to wear on me. I thought we had really made progress with Truth's narcissism, but it seems we have regressed back into her obsessing about her long since destroyed and defunct relationship with Professor Richard Rarity, Professor of Philosophy at the SWANK Institute of Technology. Time and again Truth with a capital T harks back to a golden age that never was, the supposed honeymoon period that was marked by the writing of Rarity's first major work of philosophy, Philosophy in a Hall of Mirrors.[4] *Truth beats me over the head with the same story, again and again. She recognizes this, time and again. As she says:*

> I know I keep coming back to my time with Richard during the early part of the writing of Philosophy in a Hall of Mirrors. I know that when you read the book back now it looks like he has never had any time for me, whatsoever. Yes, of course, if you look at the final, finished draft, ever more so if you look at the second and third editions in 1983 and 1991 respectively, I am clearly cast into the ghastly, disorientating hall of mirrors. Is it any wonder that Richard's abandonment has left me in a constant state of anxious and buzzing confusion? My friends—friends

---

4. As some of you will have no doubt already guessed, this is a deliberately one-dimensional and intentionally heavy-handed reference to Richard Rorty, *Philosophy and the Mirror of Nature* (Princeton, NJ: Princeton University Press, 1979). You will see a lot more reference (both explicit and implicit) to Rorty's work presently, or in this particular part of the book.

like 'language game' or 'pseudo problem'—judge me, berate me, forever
tell me that Richard's commitment to me was never serious, never real,
never even naturally felt. But, I'll tell you this, Professor Pills, they don't
know! They didn't have the same immersive experience of the earlier
drafts of the book, no idea about the seductive and flirtatious energy
between us then. The initial title Richard played around with was
*Sentimentality and Truth with a T: The Gift of the Given That Keeps
Giving.* I missed my chance at that point. I just couldn't educate him
enough to relax him long enough so that he would listen, see and then
come to desire me again. I couldn't get him to give way to my seductive
advances . . .[5]

So, we see that Professor Pills has a very specialist practice in that he only
treats concepts, but concepts with personae nonetheless, concepts that have
subjective experience, what analytic philosophers of a certain type would call
the 'fact of phenomenal consciousness', 'Qualia', or 'the what it is like to be a
Batman'.[6] The implication, or intellectual conceit of the cute bit of nonsense
articulated above (could we maybe call it a 'thought experiment' without
incurring the wrath of analytic philosophers everywhere?), is that 'there is
something it is like' for a concept to subjectively undergo experiences of
various sorts, in this case, the Truth's inner life or turmoil after a break-up
with Professor Rarity. Cute bit of nonsense or not, Mrs Pills' report of her
husband's diary entry of Monday 7th July 1997 really stopped me dead in my
tracks. I spent the rest of that day, and a significant chunk of the subsequent
day, reading and rereading the Professor Pills entries. Read back, read together,
reread and read again, the diary entries started to wear on me somewhat.

I'll provide two more examples and hopefully you will begin to get a better
sense of the wear and tear that came with reading the entries. As you will see
presently, these examples pretty much have the same structure and function
as the Rorty-inspired one above. A man, Professor Pills, says things in his
diary, a report containing observations concerning his therapy sessions on a
given day with a concept or group of concepts; a retrospective, interpretive,
even creative, re-narration of what he has seen and heard, straight (or not
so straight) from the concept's mouth. Then, a woman, Mrs Professor Pills,

---

5. Mrs Pills seems to be playing around with Rorty's often-cited suggestion from his often-cited paper 'Human Rights, Rationality and Sentimentality': namely, that 'sentimental education works only
on people who can relax long enough to listen'. See Richard Rorty, *Truth and Progress: Philosophical
Papers III* (Cambridge: Cambridge University Press, 1998), 180.
6. This would seem to be a playful attempt at humour on Kerry-Ann's part, referencing what is
perhaps the most famous essay in the philosophy of mind. See Tom Nagel, 'What Is It Like to Be a
Bat?', *The Philosophical Review* 83, no. 4 (1974): 435–50. Maybe these kinds of jokes kill at philosophy
conferences, but I personally remain unmoved.

sneaks a peek, observes and records the reporting or re-narration, providing photographic evidence of the same. So, there is an animating dynamic at play, what we could perhaps think of as a kind of linguistic or language-like redundancy that inevitably attends to the circulation of information as such. Less technically, perhaps, we might think of this as the everyday phenomenon of 'hearsay', the repeated reporting of things seen and heard, messages that are always-already socially and politically mediated through a number of voices and across various sets of circumstances.[7] Anyway, however that may be, what I want to begin to describe here is my more recent reconnection with my old PhD comrade from the 1990s (the original 'Mrs Pills' to you, dear reader). But, before that, and by way of providing a little more context, let's give those other couple of examples of diary entries.

Example 1: Monday 14th February 1998—Paradigm, the shift-worker[8]
    As the weeks and months pass, I am beginning to get ever more concerned about Paradigm. In addition to working around thirty-five hours a week as an administrative assistant in the school of dentistry at the University of Margate, Paradigm also puts in four four-hour evening shifts at Terri ('Daddy Kool') Kool's seafront bar/café. It probably doesn't help that Terri Kool is not just her boss, but an old school friend. Added to this, of course, is yet another layer of complication. For not only is Terri her boss four nights a week at Daddy Kool, but she also is the Head of the School of Dentistry at Margate. I mean, that's weird, right? What kind of self-respecting academic would want to run a seafront bar/café? Utterly bizarre! Added to this, of course, is yet another layer of complication. For Terri's business partner, 'Director of Operations' at Daddy Kool, and long-time life partner, is Mark Masterman. Is Masterman the third important point or angle of a really bizarre love triangle? From what I gather from Paradigm, Daddy Kool was initially financed and set up by Terri. She owns the business. Mark runs the day-to-day and tries to overcompensate for his junior status by acting like a big boss man with the staff (hence the ridiculous title 'Director of Operations'). Paradigm endlessly complains about the fact that Masterman seems to have it in for her, that he particularly resents her and is jealous of her longstanding friendship with Terri. Obviously, I'm no Freudian, but, at times, I just can't resist playing out various little oedipal dramas in my head in those moments when Paradigm complains about how she is treated by them. I feel for the

---

7. Immediately, I'm inclined to see this interpretive move on Kerry-Ann's part as implicitly and explicitly bringing into play Deleuze and Guattari's 'Postulates of Linguistics' as famously outlined in their book *A Thousand Plateaus*, especially knowing, as I do, that Kerry-Ann has published work in this area. See, for example, Kerry-Ann Porter and Robert Porter, 'Habermas and the Pragmatics of Communication: A Deleuze-Guattarian Critique', *Social Semiotics* 13, no. 2 (2003): 129–45.
    8. This is a rather heavy-handed, even licentious, reference to the much used and abused idea of a 'paradigm-shift'. See, obviously, Thomas Kuhn, *The Structure of Scientific Revolutions* (Chicago: University of Chicago Press, 2012). This is confirmed by Mrs Pills below in conversation with Kerry-Ann.

poor girl, but she drives me crazy as she seems to have no will to get herself out of this. She ignores all my really good practical advice on how to develop variously useful techniques of self-care in stressful work situations. I even gave her a copy of my latest self-care book (Techniques of Self-Care: Your Journey to Workplace Wellness Starts Here!) *at a good discount, 15 per cent. When I quizzed her about the book during our sessions it was clear she hadn't bothered to look at it, complaining that she simply didn't have the time. Damn it, she won't even follow my instructions regarding the anxiety/depression medication I've prescribed. I feel for the poor girl, I do. I know this sounds terribly paternal, even harsh, but she really needs to start doing what I am telling her to do. Today, for instance, I asked her a simple question about her medication: 'So, Paradigm, in our last session we agreed that we would increase your dose, yes? So, do you think it has helped?' Her response to me was all over the place and I never would have been able to recount it for the diary if I hadn't already pressed the red 'record' button on my Dictaphone:*

Professor Pills, I dunno what to tell you! I'm just going round and round in circles. Paradigm do this, Paradigm do that . . .

You remember I was telling you about this big academic conference last year that Terri had me involved in: 'The Structure of Dental Revolutions'.[9] There was over 150 delegates, about eight or nine keynote speakers, however many panels, food, hotels, excursions, social events and all sorts. Just because we are 'old friends', just because Terri always says shit like the reason I'm asking you to do all these supposedly 'important' things is because I trust you and you're the best, better than the others in the school office . . . It's bullshit. She's working me over because she knows she can get away with it. Some fucking friend, huh?

And if that's not enough, I've got to spend four nights a week eating shit from her jealous and insecure man, Masterman. Shrivel dick loser! Terri knows that I know if I say no to her at my regular day job, that my night shifts at Daddy Kool will get cut. She has done that before. She knows I need those hours. She knows I'm trying to raise two teenage boys on my own. Mark knows all this too, of course. Fuck, they really have me over a barrel . . .

One minute I'm the one and only Paradigm to Terri because I do what good old Paradigm does. The next minute Masterman convinces Terri that we need to put old Paradigm to work in a whole bunch of other ways (twenty-two at last count). Not just at Daddy Kool by the way! But at the university as well! I mean what the fuck does Mark have to do with what happens in our school office? But, she'll say to me, 'Oh, you know, Mark and I were talking last night about such and such and we wondered whether you wanted to help me do bla bla bla . . . '

---

9. Just in case you hadn't already got the Kuhn reference. That actually did amuse me.

I mean the latest thing I've been roped into is a series of follow-up seminars to the 'The Structure of Dental Revolutions' conference. Terri calls it an important 'postscript' to all the 'great work we did together with the conference'. Nightmare! So, no longer should I be doing the Paradigm thing as Paradigm. I have to perform and be all these other things that I've never been before. All of sudden, I'm expected to be a 'disciplinary matrix'. For it seems like being old Paradigm is just not good enough anymore. Then it turns out that that's not even good enough. Coz I then have to become a 'symbolic generalization', then a 'belief in particular models', 'values', and then an 'exemplar'.[10] Honest to Christ, it just never ends . . .

I think I am going to have to take sick leave.
Can you give me a sick line?

Example 2: Friday 11th April 1998—Survival, the Freelance worker[11]
I'm concerned about Survival's future, about her future becoming nothing other than an unhealthily obsessive concern about the future. At the beginning, I thought the real danger was burnout. She would sometimes complain about the dizziness that came with the freedom of being a freelancer, being 'her own boss', as she like to put it, but most of time she seemed to giddily luxuriate in the liberty of a work life freely chosen. Of course, we now know that such talk about dizzying freedom was uncannily prescient because over recent months her anxiety disorder has been consistently presenting as vertigo, rather than the insomnia that prompted her to become my patient

---

10. This not only amused me, but, more importantly perhaps, had my reaching for my copy of Kuhn's *Structure* and indeed some of the relevant secondary literature on it. Now, over seventy years on from its original publication in the early 1960s, it is perhaps hard for us to fully appreciate the furore it created when it first came out. Clearly, Mrs Pills knows a bit about the text and about the context of its reception. Allow me to try to explain. That man 'Masterman' refers to one of key initial responses to *Structure* by a woman called Margaret Masterman. In a well-known and influential collection edited by Imre Lakatos and Alan Musgrave, *Criticism and the Growth of Knowledge* (Cambridge: Cambridge University Press, 1970), Masterman published a paper, 'The Nature of a Paradigm', in which she draws attention to the variously distinct ways in which Kuhn put the notion of 'paradigm' to work in *Structure*. She counted twenty-one all told. Interestingly, in the fragment of *Academic World* quoted above, we have 'Paradigm the shift-worker' complaining that she has been put to work in *twenty-two different ways*. This, surely, is a knowing nod to the fact that while much cited, not least by Kuhn himself in his 'postscript' (note the term 'postscript' appears in quotations in the entry here) to *Structure*, Masterman is mistakenly read by her more illustrious interlocutor as Kuhn often repeats and accepts the criticism that he uses the term 'paradigm' in twenty-two distinct ways, a concession that forced him to famously lament that he had completely 'lost control' of the concept. 'Big whoop' I can almost hear you say! So, he mistakenly misquoted Masterman by saying twenty-two rather than twenty-one? Well, I mention all this seemingly unnecessary detail because I think it is indicative of the fact that although the diary entries we find in *Academic World* are deliberately and intentionally rather one-dimensional and heavy handed (a point that the real Mrs Pills makes in conversation with Kerry-Ann below), they nonetheless spring from a good working knowledge of the concepts, scholars, and famous works they reference. My point being simply this: The popular idiom of the zine shouldn't blind us to the conceptual work going on here.

11. As you will see confirmed below, the key textual reference in this entry is Raoul Vaneigem, *The Revolution of Everyday Life* (London: Rebel Press, 2006).

in the first instance. More and more Survival talks about her freelance projects as so many things she is 'holding together in tension'. This phrase—'holding together in tension'—has become something of a discursive trope, a recurrent theme, a constant refrain, a motif that patterns her increasingly scatty, muddled, even anxiously incoherent, descriptions of her everyday work life. I initially thought that her acceptance of a permanent 0.4 lectureship in furniture design at the Five Cocks School of Arts in Five Cocks was a positive development. I thought this role would have given her some steady and guaranteed income without risking the kind of 'institutionalization' she dreaded (I do wonder why the term 'institutionalization' so effortlessly seems to trip off her tongue at least ten to fifteen times a session?). I thought that because she told me so. She would often explicitly report that the balance between the regular income generated through teaching two-and-a-bit days per week at Five Cocks and her two-and-a-bit days in the studio creatively designing her furniture pieces was the 'best of all possible worlds'. In the end, though, she took to saying it so often that it naturally made 'methink the lady doth protest too much!'. As with a number of my other younger female clients, I've taken to recording my sessions with Survival. Ethical problems notwithstanding, it is vital that I have some mechanism for recording conversational talk and interactional behaviour in a way that secures the most comprehensive understanding. How else am I supposed to judge her, or indeed any other of my clients? I mean how could I be expected to make any sense of the fragment of talk reproduced below? Today, in response to my usual opening salvo ('Well, Survival, how have things been going?'), she immediately went off the rails:

I've become the very thing I've always despised CW! I mean you called me on it. I've become a . . . 'sucker'. How did you put it a few weeks ago? Something about Nietzsche and 'loving the poison that kills you', wasn't it? Anyway, you know! You're the last person I'd have to explain it to! But I have to keep reminding myself, you know? I have to keep reminding myself that I built the maze I can't get out of. Ha, just like Flav from PE.[12] Sorry, you wouldn't get that reference. He's like Nietzsche, but with a big clock hanging round his neck. Ha, imagine that! Nietzsche with a big clock? You know a friend once saw Flav and the rest of Public Enemy at Heathrow airport and she saw him at the security bit putting the clock through those machines they have. Hilarious!

Anyway, what was I saying? Yeah, I'm a sucker! You know friends of mine, people, like me, who did their PhDs in art history in the early 90s at our beloved alma mater, they're all out there doing their thing as proper academics! They work in decent institutions, they teach about half the amount I do, getting paid more than twice as much. They have time to do their pet projects and research, to go to conferences, to have proper down time and holidays in Summer, without having to worry about money. But not me! I was better than them. I wasn't going to

---

12. This is a play on lyrics from a *Public Enemy* song: 'Can't Do Nuttin' for Ya Man!'.

waste my privilege or my parents' money on a boring academic career. I have to remind myself of my arrogance, my arrogant desire to view myself as above them. What the fuck happened? Did I read some arty-cum-political book, eat a dodgy kebab before bed, and wake up the next morning an aspiring revolutionary? Academia was for other people, like my friends, boring people, people on the predictable treadmill, people on the instalment plan. That wasn't me! I was an artist after all! I was a poet. My designs were going to rearrange the furniture in people's head, create the kind of felt sensations they had never had before, a poetry of the everyday, a poetical revolution of everyday life.

I mean, ah fuck, I dunno what I mean . . .

As I sat in my office that day, reading diary entry after diary entry, the arrogance, stupidity, and misogyny of Professor Pills began to really impress itself on me, again. I say 'again' because it seems I had totally forgotten the original political impulse animating 'The secret diary of Professor C Wright Pills, aged 44¼'. This really bothered me. This was precisely why I was moved to reconnect to my old PhD comrade, to talk again about the things we experienced back there and then, maybe even to understand better, in retrospect, what it was we were trying to do with *Academic World*. My old comrade (let's stick with the pseudonym 'Mrs Pills') and I had barely spoken in years. From time to time we would exchange an email, a DM on Twitter, or comment on each other's Facebook posts. But we weren't friends anymore, at least in the non-Facebook sense. Of course, being friends on Facebook meant that we were able to follow each other's lives from a distance. For instance, I knew that after she defended her PhD she went to work at a university in the south of England as a lecturer in philosophy, before then moving to Scotland for a period, and finally settling out where she is now. I knew that like me she had two daughters, both in their teens. All the distance we had travelled, yet we kind of found ourselves in a similar place, albeit on opposite sides of the world. After a few DMs on Twitter, we managed finally to schedule a Zoom call at a time that suited us both (not easy when you consider the time difference between where she is now and where I'm based). Anyway, one Zoom call became three Zoom calls, became a regular Zoom call, became what I'm tempted to call a real or genuine reconnection and friendship, in the non-Facebook sense. What I am going to reproduce below is a transcript of fragments of some of these Zoom calls. Unlike Professor Pills, I explicitly sought permission from my friend to record the Zoom calls. It was clear after our initial reconnection or catch-up call that I needed to have some way to record in detail our conversations. This was specifically the case, given that she, Mrs Pills, is a trained philosopher and I, alas, am not. What is documented below are not verbatim transcriptions, but slightly cleaner versions, something that tries to make the dialogue between us as perspicuous as possible.

〰

Kerry-Ann Porter (KAP). 'Reading back the Professor Pills diary entries from *Academic World*, and knowing how philosophically well-read you are, I am always left feeling I'm not quite getting the full implications of what is being said. So, I'll begin with a simple question. Where did the idea come from? For instance, there seems to be an obvious reference to Sue Townsend's well-known *Secret Diary of Adrian Mole*?[13] But, maybe that's too obvious?'

Mrs Pills (Mrs P). 'Ha, yeah!' You know, I really hadn't clocked that at the time and I don't think I was trying to make a specific point. Of course, I knew of the existence of the book, but maybe I've simply plagiarized it without giving it any thought whatsoever. Although I could see how one could read it as a reference to a set of self-absorbed, adolescent, narcissistic musings. To be honest, I think the literary or cultural backcloth to it was much more high-brow and elevated [laughs]. Obviously, and as you've already implied, you know my intellectual background. I'm an "analytic" philosopher by training, whatever that may mean nowadays. You know that part of my thesis work was on Richard Rorty's notion of philosophy as a kind of therapy, something he articulated with such provocation and startling brilliance in *Philosophy in the Mirror of Nature*. The references to this are pretty consistent and obvious when you look back at diary entries. At that time, I was completely smitten with Rorty'.

KAP. 'So, [laughs] what was it about Rorty that made you such a smitten kitten?'

Mrs P. 'I know, imagine that! But I think it was his style of argumentation. The way he seemed to cut through the pomposity and pretentiousness of philosophy, his ability to democratize ideas, to somehow connect philosophy to social and political life in a way that seemed neither cumbersome nor forced, but rather pressing and pertinent'.

---

13. *The Secret Diary of Adrian Mole, Aged 13¾* is the first book in a series of comedies written by Sue Townsend. Written and set in the UK of the early 1980s, this first set of diaries, while undoubtedly played for laughs and while poor Adrian is often the butt of the joke, are nonetheless, at times, quite excoriating of the early Thatcherite government of the time.

KAP. 'What the hell are you talking about?'

Mrs P. 'C'mon KA, I'm pouring my heart out here [laughs]. Look, think of it like this, OK? Philosophy is a disease, right, a kind of obsessive-compulsive disorder. So, what does the obsessive-compulsive philosophical desire amount to? Well, my argument in the thesis (and I still think that this might be something I'd want to defend if pushed) was that philosophy suffers from a kind of debilitating and degenerative catholic fallibility. There is a kind of stain, call it original sinfulness if you like, that philosophers inherit at birth. They seem to have to bear any number of debts, and precisely the kind of debts that they will never be able to pay off. Maybe you remember me constantly rabbiting on about a "Jargon of Indebtedness" as a plague on contemporary philosophy? Anyway, in the thesis, I would tend to connect such notions of "debt" or "indebtedness" to what I call the "big picture philosophy obsessions" or, in more common terms, "the perennial problems of philosophy". So, things like; the "mind-body problem", the "free-will-determinism problem", and so on . . . Now, what's great about Rorty (and he gets better and better at this the older he gets; for example, in the mid-career works that he is more famous for like *Contingency, Irony and Solidarity*, and *Achieving Our Country*) is that he sets all this "big picture" or "perennial problem" stuff aside. Look, and this is the most important point here, he sets it aside in a therapeutic gesture that amounts to living with and through it, even if a little obsessively for a while. He lives and relives his obsession with the "big problems" of philosophy with his therapist (not a real living breathing one, like our friend Professor Pills, but the philosophical interlocutors that pepper a book like *Philosophy and the Mirror of Nature*—giants of the tradition like Descartes and Locke, or his analytic contemporaries like Wilfrid Sellars, Thomas Kuhn and so on . . .). A simple, straightforward declaration of one's ignorance of the sins of one's philosophical fathers is not enough for him. To simply and smugly state one's indifference to the false or pseudo problems bequeathed to us by the history of philosophy is a gesture that will always fall short. You have to *do* the history of philosophy, to foreground the contingency and particularity of the philosophical story. Only then will you be able to understand it, understand the category mistakes, the wrong turns, the historical dead-ends, the forks in the road, the roads we never travelled, the roads we could have travelled or still might travel, the cul-de-sacs, the needless and pointless obsessions that you would have been better off never thinking about. Only then will your way of doing philosophy, thinking about philosophy, have some kind of curative effect'.

KAP. 'All joking aside, I'm not really sure I'm following you here. As a student, I obviously came across some of Rorty's work (you just mentioned

Contingency, Irony and Solidarity, Achieving Our Country—those middle or "political" works, if you like). Aren't these books more than a little bit smug? I seem to remember reading Rorty in those contexts and thinking that, actually, he too quickly dismissed those he disagreed with, that he could have better shown the kind of critical-historical consciousness that you were just praising him for. But, look, I'm not interested in talking about Richard Rorty. I'm interested in hearing you talk about the political impulse behind what you were doing at the time we were producing *Academic World*'.

Mrs P. 'Don't you see the link? Don't you remember?'

KAP. 'Remember what? Obviously, I don't. What are you hinting at?'

Mrs P. 'Remember all the trouble I had with the guy who shall remain nameless?'

KAP. 'Yes, I do, but do you really want to talk about that?'

Mrs P. 'No, I really do not. But there is a point to be made here, in a more abstract sort of way'.

KAP. 'What kind of point?'

Mrs P. 'Before I say something about that I'm going to have to come back on your critique of Rorty. I mean, your suggestion that he is somehow smug and lacking in historical consciousness . . .'

KAP. 'Christ the night, you're relentless. You're right, philosophers are diseased!'

Mrs P. [laughs]. 'Yep. Anyway, any smugness, and any lack of historical consciousness found in Rorty's work from the that middle period—*Contingency, Irony, Solidarity, Achieving Our Country*, etc.—is very much cast in a new light if you go back and read a book like *Philosophy and the Mirror of Nature*, or even the essays from the 1970s and early 1980s that make up a book like *Consequences of Pragmatism*.[14] These texts are more detailed, much more alive to problem of historicity, to the notion that the history of philosophy is always a kind of history of winners, you know, something retrospectively revised in the image of those who come to dominate. So, and here's my partial defence of Rorty (I say partial because you do have a point); if the project in *Philosophy and the Mirror of Nature* is, at least in part, to cure oneself of the obsessive philosophical disease of needless worrying about problems you shouldn't worry about, or problems that are not really problems, or problems that are simply too trivial to detain you, then he achieved that, at least in

14. See Richard Rorty, *Contingency, Irony, and Solidarity* (Cambridge: Cambridge University Press, 1989); Richard Rorty, *Achieving Our Country: Leftist Thought in Twentieth-Century America* (Cambridge, MA: Harvard University Press, 1999); Richard Rorty, *Consequences of Pragmatism* (Minneapolis: University of Minnesota Press, 1982); Richard Rorty, *Philosophy and the Mirror of Nature* (Princeton: Princeton University Press, 1979).

a way. He never went back there. But he used the lessons learned in this formative work to inform his developing philosophy, particularly the kind of political philosophy you would know him for'.

KAP. 'OK, I'll have a look at *Philosophy and the Mirror of Nature*'.

Mrs P. 'You should!'

KAP. 'So, can we get back on point?'

Mrs P. 'Oooh, on point? You're starting to sound like a diseased philosopher! What point?'

KAP. 'Christ, the point you hinted at above. The abstract point that speaks to the thing—he who should remain nameless—you don't want to speak of'.

Mrs P. [laughs] 'Oh, yeah I forgot about that. Let me come at it this way . . . Oh, before I do, what diary entries in particular have you recently read?'

KAP. 'I read all of them. But the three I kept going back to were: 1. "Truth with a capital T"; 2. "Paradigm, the shift worker"; 3. "Survival, the freelance worker"'.

Mrs P. 'OK, so our friend Rorty ("Truth with a capital T"), obviously, then Thomas Kuhn ("Paradigm, the shift worker") and a bit of a random one for me, the Situationist Raoul Vaneigem ("Survival, the freelance worker"). Vaneigem is probably the only thinker referenced who wasn't in some way connected to my preoccupation with "analytic" philosophy at the time. I guess the nod to Vaneigem was me doffing my cap to the folks at *Processed World*, a way of acknowledging the influence of Vaneigem's *The Revolution of Everyday Life* on what they were trying to do. They plagiarized Vaneigem, we plagiarized them. All's fair in love and plagiarism, I guess . . .'

KAP. 'Oh crikey, I should have been more alive to the Vaneigem stuff! Of course, I see it now—his notion of "survival sickness", the ideological promise of a form of gratification that is endlessly deferred. Shit, now that I look at it again, I see you actually use his language of the "instalment plan" there. How did I forget that? My memory is getting worse. Isn't it a real shame people don't think about or write about Vaneigem these days?'

Mrs P. 'I dunno, is it? [laughs] By the way, your memory has always been awful. In a way, of course, the diary entries are about memory. Or, maybe better put, they are about recording and observing things. Better still, they connect to the notion of "observation reports". In a certain kind of "analytic" philosophy there is a lot of talk about "observation reports", not just in Rorty's early work, but in the work of other analytic philosophers that shaped his thinking. For example, earlier I mentioned Wilfrid Sellars . . .'

KAP. 'Of course, one of the entries is about Sellars isn't it? It's coming back to me now . . . Wasn't there something about a patient/concept call "Myth" who was concerned that she was too "giving" or something?'

Mrs P. 'Yeah, that's right, [laughs] I was lazily channelling the famous Sellarsian notion of the "myth of the given", probably not one of my better ones, eminently forgettable actually (never really got my head around Sellars to be honest). Anyway, the point about all the entries was to capture or illustrate two related notions. Or, maybe it would be better to say, in the terms of the question you asked earlier, that the political impulse has something to do with trying to get at two related things. First, the supposed sterility of observation reports that are anything but sterile. I suppose if I read trendy "French Theory" I'd say that Professor Pills is libidinally invested in recording his experience with his subjects, a kind of voyeurism that is lived out most vicariously *after* the event, where and when he gets to judge his patients in the absence of any comeback or challenge. At some points, of course, I imagine C Wright justifying his behaviour to himself ("it's important for me to secretly record my patients to better understand their problems, etc. . . . ."), but that's not treated seriously at all. He is purposively as one dimensional as the supposedly one-dimensional women/concepts he describes. So, it's always crude! No-one in their right mind could read these entries and think Professor Pills was a good guy, right?'

KAP. 'I could! I had a bit of sympathy for him in the beginning, having to listen to all these fucked-up women'. [laughs]

Mrs P. 'Don't talk shit! I mean even the most misogynist dickhead couldn't fail to see that Professor Pills was a rather dodgy customer'.

KAP. 'You'd be surprised! Seriously, it took a while for the impression of his dickheadedness to really sink in. Sorry, I interrupted. What was the second thing you wanted to say by way of the political impulse informing the entries?'

Mrs P. 'Well, it's kind of the thing you raised earlier, a sort of smugness and lack of contextual understanding. Both things are possibly related, I think. Look, think of it this way: the abstract sterility of the "observation reports" as related or enveloped in a kind of secret or walled-off moment of de-contextualized representation (the nightly, masturbatory, ritual of writing up the entries). So, he is a bad therapist, and for good Rortian reasons. You know what I mean?'

KAP. 'I'm afraid you've lost me again. Do you mean he is a bad therapist because he judges concepts in the abstract and in private? Or, is it that he overly psychologizes and individualizes their situation? So, for instance, he gives "Paradigm, the shift worker" his wonderful self-help book at a discount, checks on her medication, but refuses to engage with the historical situatedness of her experience; the organizational, economic, social, and political conditions shaping things? Perhaps it is something to do with the fact he is not prepared to be challenged by the concepts, to live and act with them to achieve some curative end together? Is that what makes him a bad therapist from a Rortian perspective? Oh boy, you've really sucked me in here. I'm talking some serious bollox now . . .'

Mrs P. 'Yep, you really are talking some very serious bollox now!' [laughs]

KAP. 'Seriously, help me out here, would you?'

Mrs P. 'Why is this so important? Let me turn the tables and ask you; why are you motivated to revisit the *Academic World* days? Is it to do with this book you're writing? That's what I'm assuming, right?'

KAP. 'Of course, yes!'

Mrs P. 'So, what is it that you want me to say here? You're asking me to help you out, but I'm not sure with what exactly . . .'

KAP. 'Christ, I'm not sure myself . . .' [laughs]

Mrs P. 'Look, why don't we stop now, catch up in a week or so? That'll give you time to think about it. I know you're going to take the piss, but maybe it would help to come up with two or three themes or propositions to help anchor our next discussion?'

KAP. 'You mean turn it into one of your philosophy seminars when you get to show off how much smarter you are than me?'

Mrs P. 'Yes, exactly!' [laughs]

KAP. 'Knew it! OK, same time next week suit you?'

Mrs P. 'Yep, see you then . . .'

KAP. 'You'll be impressed to know that I was a good girl and did my homework as requested'.

Mrs P. 'Wha . . .'

KAP. 'I've come up with themes for our discussion'.

Mrs P. 'Ohhhh, good girl . . .' [overenthusiastically, speedily, sarcastically claps her hands]

KAP. 'Smart arse! Anyway . . .'

Mrs P. 'Hold on, let me get my best Andorran pen to write these gems down . . .'

KAP. 'Shut it, will you! Right, first, I guess I'm interested in the institutional and organizational backdrop to our production of *Academic World*. Obviously, I've been doing a lot of background reading on the contemporary university. There's a lot of academic work out there, much more than I thought there would be . . .'.

Mrs P. 'What? You're surprised that academics would write about themselves and their own situation. Read the room, girlfriend . . .'

KAP. 'Stop bloody interrupting me, would you?'

Mrs P. 'Sorry, couldn't resist that one . . .' [laughs]

KAP. 'What was I saying . . .'

Mrs P. '. . . the abundance of academic literature on the academy . . .'

KAP. 'You're doing it again . . .'

Mrs P. 'Sorry, but . . .' [laughs]

KAP. 'Oh dear . . . this is going to be a long Zoom call tonight . . .'

KAP. 'Right, the first theme is to do with the "observation reports" you mentioned before. Don't laugh, but since our last chat I actually tried to read a bit of Rorty's *Philosophy and the Mirror of Nature* and even a bit of Sellars' *Empiricism and the Philosophy of Mind* . . .'

Mrs P. 'Really? Where's that Andorran pen again?' [laughs]

KAP. 'Hey, I'm even going to quote a bit of *Empiricism and the Philosophy of Mind* to you. Listen to this, it's from the section entitled "Does Empirical Knowledge Have a Foundation?" Weirdly, the paragraphs are numbered here. Is that an "analytic" thing? Anyway, don't answer that! I have typed up these notes, so I can share screen with you here. Hopefully you can see it. This is the fragment of paragraph 38 that I would like to read to you:

> The idea that observation . . . is constituted by certain self-authenticating nonverbal episodes, the authority of which is transmitted to verbal or quasi-verbal performances when these performances are made 'in conformity with the semantic rules of the language' is, of course, the heart of the Myth of the Given. For the *given*, in epistemological tradition, is what is *taken* by these self-authenticating episodes. These 'takings' are, so to speak, the unmoved movers of empirical knowledge, the 'knowings in presence' which are presupposed by all other knowledge . . . Such is the framework in which traditional empiricism makes its characteristic claim that the perceptually given is the foundation of empirical knowledge.[15]

Now, this is really interesting to me. So, by talking about "self-authenticating nonverbal episodes" being "transmitted to verbal or quasi-verbal performances" I'm assuming that he means someone, somewhere seeing something and then saying something to confirm its meaning and significance'.

Mrs P. Well, not . . .'

KAP. 'No, let me finish. Or, better, let's think about a concrete example. Let's think about the kind of nonverbal episode that might imprint itself on the mind, an event witnessed in such and such a place and time, confined to

---

15. Wilfrid Sellars, *Empiricism and the Philosophy of Mind* (Cambridge, MA: Harvard University Press, 1997), 77.

memory, yet one that constantly bubbles up. Let's say it's a memory of 1990s academia and I see a slightly sleazy older male academic resting his grubby little hand on the back of one of his young female PhD students.'

Mrs P. 'OK, I think I see where you're going with this . . .'

KAP. 'No wait, just let me finish. Let's say the hand rests there for what seems an inordinate length of time. Let's say that image, of the hand that won't move, imprints itself on the mind of the perceiver in question, stays with the perceiver, indeed connects that perceiver to the fellow female PhD student perceived. Let's say there is a certain kind of solidarity established by way of the perception because the perceiver recognizes herself, her own situation, in the perceived, most particularly, in the uncomfortable squirmy negotiation her peer is forced into as a consequence of the inappropriate behaviour of the older sleazy male . . .'

Mrs P. 'Not sure I'm following here. Well, of course, I'm following you all too literally because it's about THAT time and about you know WHO, and clearly about our friendship as fellow PhD students being established or grounded in a shared experience of what the kids today would call "everyday sexism", sorry, "hashtageverydaysexism" [laughs]. But, I'm at a loss to see how, and in what productive way, this connects to Willfrid Sellars? Are you looking to do a kind of feminist critique of Sellars? I'd imagine that would imply delving into his biography. I have some vague sense he was married more than once and was a bit of a drinker . . .'

KAP. 'Ha, no, nothing like that. Though, funny you mention it, I did read some stuff online about his drinking. It seems he was a pretty "high-functioning" boozer [laughs]. I also read somewhere that "pink ice cubes" would often appear as objects of concern in his theoretical or philosophical papers on perception, thereby perhaps echoing the everyday fact of his boozing while writing.[16] No, what I guess I'm really interested in, and what the rereading of *Academic World* and our conversations in particular have vividly brought to mind, is the problem of the *reliability* of these things we have calling "observation reports"; that is, how "observation reports" work, or gain traction, in certain settings. I guess if I was going to return your hashtageverydaysexism serve with a hashtag of my own, I'd probably call it hashtageverydaysexismintheacademy. At the end of our last Zoom meeting you asked me what was motivating me to revisit the *Academic World* days. More than anything else, this is what is motivating me I think: a desire to talk about this stuff, and the problem of finding the right way of talking about it, if that makes sense?'

---

16. See, for example, Wilfrid Sellars 'Sensa or Sensings: Reflections on the Ontology of Perception,' *Philosophical Studies* (Essays in Honor of James Cornman) 41 (1982): 83–111.

Mrs P. 'So what are you getting from Sellars in this context? On the face of it, it would seem a rather odd choice to zero in on him. You do realize that he would want to epistemologically problematize the nature of the episode or event in question. Crudely put, he would want to say that the perceptual, nonverbal apprehension of "male sleaziness" (whatever that could mean?) would need to be treated very delicately if you are to avoid falling prey to the Myth of the Given?'

KAP. 'Yes, exactly!'

Mrs P. 'Yes, exactly?'

KAP. 'OK, shut up and listen. Don't interrupt me. Let me try to get this out in as coherent a fashion as I can. I think it is precisely the Sellarsian idea of challenging the kind of naive empiricism that attends to "looking", and how we talk about "looks" and "looking", that we need to focus in on. Listen, think about this! I was thinking about my mum! Born in the mid-1940s and got her first job in a cigarette factory in the 1960s. She had her first child in 1965. She had to leave her job. She had her second child in 1969. She had to again leave the job she left in 1965. She had her third child (me) in 1973. Yes, you've guessed it . . .

Now, when I talk to her about that, when I tell how horrendous and immoral I think that was, she will, if not defend the cigarette company she worked for, at least try to explain it away with some vague phrase like "well that's what it was like then, Kerry-Ann" or "well at least they took me back, after I had you, and they didn't have to, you know". More injuriously, the same kind of vibe emanates from her when she recalls what we would now clearly consider clear explicit victimisation and abuse. I'll tell you one story, really quickly. It involved one of her supervisors in the cigarette factory, let's call him "Jack". Actually, she used to refer to him as a bit of a "Jack the lad", but it took me quite a while to appreciate what she meant by that description. In my head, a "Jack the lad" is a bloke's bloke, a bit full of himself, and often without much cause to be. A bit of a dick, but mainly harmless. This Jack was a dick no doubt, but he was far from harmless.

Basically, Jack used to go around "feeling up", as Mum would say, any woman on the factory floor that he fancied. Now, the way my mum talks about this is really interesting, if more than a little disturbing and somewhat discombobulating. Essentially there are three categories of women that emerge in this kind of talk, defined by how they responded to "Jack". First, there were the women who ignored it, who pretended he wasn't there, pretended until he actually wasn't there anymore. Mum put herself in that camp, the women who treated him as "invisible", as somehow beneath their notice. Second, there were the women who more or less reluctantly went along with it, brushing it off as a kind of "harmless banter", as Mum would say. Third, there were a few, but very much a minority, who physically stood up to him or complained to the other supervisors or the union (though it didn't help that "Jack" himself was a union rep). Now—and here is where things getting even more curious or strange—implicit in this narrative and categorization of the differing responses is a moral-political hierarchy of sorts. Perhaps unsurprisingly, at the bottom are the women who indulged Jack and participated in the "banter". Women like that, my mum would say, were complicit in the reproduction of the "banter": indeed, some of them, she speculated, may have even practically encouraged it. Simply put, their complicity implies responsibility here, maybe even culpability in some cases. In the middle are the small minority of women who stood up to Jack, who complained, who, as my mum would put, "kicked up a stink" or "made a big fuss". While my Mum admired their guts on the one hand, on the other hand, she would simultaneously admonish them for "kicking up a stink". Why? Well, her thinking here has a "realpolitik" flavour to it. "Kicking up a stink" never got the women anywhere, or so she argued. They were ignored. Worse still, it actually made things more awkward as the other supervisors and the union guys the women actually complained to (all men, obviously) were mates with Jack and were only too happy to see things from their buddy's per-spective. I don't even think it is right to say Jack's mates "covered" for him, or "brushed it under the carpet". The simple reason being that there is no need to cover for someone if they haven't done anything wrong as such. As far as they were concerned, he simply hadn't done anything wrong. This is why the various petty little retributions visited not just on the women who complained, but all the women on the factory floor, were, in a sense, justified in their heads. They were a justified response to those women engaged in "trouble-making" or "rabble rousing", when they should have just been getting on with their work'.

Mrs P. 'Bonkers . . .'

KAP. 'Is it, though?'

Mrs P. 'What do you mean? Of course it's bonkers, the victim blaming, doubling down on the abuse. Even how your mum frames it; as a moral-political hierarchy of victim blaming? I mean, come on. Are you seriously telling me that some of the women really encouraged this "Jack" fucker?'

KAP. 'But, hang on a minute! For the hermeneutical distance that sepa-rates our shared experiences in academia (whether back in the 90s when we were PhD students or even right now a fifth of the way through the twenty-first century) is not perhaps as intergalactic as we might like to think'.

Mrs P. 'C'mon, Kerry-Ann. You can't seriously suggest . . .'

KAP. 'Well, sorry to interrupt, but just let me follow the story a bit more before you come to a more definitive judgement. Let me come back to Mum's category of women to finish the moral-political hierarchy. These are the women who would treat "Jack" as invisible, as merely an irritant too insignificant and lowly to even merit responding to. Mum's implicit suggestion that they come out top of her moral-political hierarchy rests on two assumptions. The first one is a kind of stoic matriarchal one. People like "Jack" are like toddlers who misbehave to elicit a reaction. They are attention seekers, and the worst thing you can do is respond. You respond and the situation escalates proportionately (hence the critique of the small minority who "kicked up a stink" and the realpolitik recognition of how such action gives rise to petty retributions effecting all the women). You ignore, you remain impassive, you treat the lowly, grubby little male sleaze-ball as an unruly toddler not worth your time or indulgence, then things deescalate. The second assumption is something like a pragmatic or realist one. The thought here is that there is no point in ever speaking out about something—even if it is something you really feel, perceive, or otherwise experience in some way—if you do not have the right kind of language to do so, the appropriate kind of talk that will make a difference or effect change. There's nothing to say when you have nothing you can say! This brings me back to Sellars . . .'

Mrs P. 'Wait, what?'

KAP. 'I know this sounds all a bit strange. I guess what I'm trying to do is to give you a feel for the experience I have when I talk to my Mum about this stuff. There is a weird circularity to our exchanges. Mum is vaguely aware of the hermeneutic distance that critically plays back against her talk of the 1960s factory floor and how we might view that dim and distant social world in the here and now, a critical perspective that is no doubt a product of her conversations with me over the years. She tells me how it was. I tell her how ridiculous, horrible, and horrendous her story sounds. Further, I admonish her for her victim blaming and her inability to see how she has "internalized the patriarchy", or whatever. So, of course, I agree with you about the weirdness and problematic nature of Mum's moral and political hierarchy of responses. Yes, yes, yes, she, of course, is missing the point that emphasizing the responses of the women rather than the unchecked abuses of "Jack" is, simply, crazy. Of course, it is, it absolutely is. Yet, and here is the kicker, she will then admonish herself, criticize herself, at my righteously indignant urging. I'll condescend and say things like "How could you not speak out"? It took me a long while to realize that all I was achieving with this type of intemperate and moralizing talk was the inculcation of a guilt in Mum that simply hadn't been felt before. I blamed her, for being, I dunno, a bad feminist or something. Not a bad feminist exactly, but a nonfeminist, if you know what I mean'.

Mrs P. 'How did that go down with her?'

KAP. 'Well, most of the time she would de-escalate, ignore the annoying and intemperate toddler preaching at her . . .'

Mrs P. 'Nice one! I can definitely see the benefits of that strategy . . . [laughs]. OK, bring it back to Sellars then . . .'

KAP. 'OK. Let me quote another passage from *Empiricism and the Philosophy of Mind*. This is earlier in the text. I don't know if you remember, but this is the bit in the text where he tells the story about a guy who works in a tie shop, how he learns not by simple observation, but by inference, that the colour of the necktie is blue rather than green . . .'

Mrs P. 'Oh yes, sorry to interrupt, but those stories are really nutty, really fun. People talk about the dramatic, flowery, literary style of so called "continental philosophy", but the kind of "analytic philosophy" we find in Sellars, and in what comes after him, is chock full of weird stories, thought experiments, intuition pumps, zombies, robots, speculations concerning whether the Chinese nation has a functionalist consciousness . . .'[17]

KAP. 'What the fuck you talking about?'

Mrs P. [laughs] 'Sorry, hit me with your Sellars quote, go on . . .'

KAP. 'I am actually going to give you a few long quotes now—extra punishment for interrupting me again. Here's the first one; from section/paragraphs 15 and 16. Sellars writes:

Let me begin by noting that there certainly seems to be something to the idea that the sentence 'This looks green to me now' has a reporting role. Indeed, it would seem to be essentially a report. But, if so, *what* does it report, if not a minimal objective fact . . . to be analysed in terms of sense data?

Let me next call attention to the fact that the experience of having something look green to one at a certain time is, insofar as it is an experience, obviously very much like that of seeing something to be green, insofar as the latter is an experience. But the latter, of course, is not *just* an experience. And this is the heart of the matter. For to say that a certain experience is a *seeing that* something is the case, is to do more than describe that experience. It is to

---

17. We find 'zombies', 'robots', 'intuition pumps', 'China brains' aplenty in late twentieth-century and early twenty-first century 'philosophy of mind'. For a good survey of this very weird academic subspecialism, see one of its nuttiest exponents; namely, David Chalmers, ed., *Philosophy of Mind: Classical and Contemporary Readings* (Oxford: Oxford University Press, 2002). Of course, we now know from our current historical vantage point (late 2033) that this subspecialism of philosophy of mind has pretty much been made redundant by developments in neuroscience. See, most famously, Tiesj Benoot, *The Folk-Psychological Implosion of Philosophy of Mind: Toward a Neuroscientific Critique* (Oudenaarde: Flandrian Press, 2029).

characterize it as, so to speak, making an assertion or claim and—which is the point I wish to stress—to *endorse* that claim.[18]

Right, now what if I replaced the word "green" in the above passage with the word "sleazy" or the word "inappropriate" or the word "unlawful"? Here, look, I'll first share screen with the term *sleazy* cut and paste in:

> Let me begin by noting that there certainly seems to be something to the idea that the sentence 'This looks **sleazy** to me now' has a reporting role. Indeed, it would seem to be essentially a report. But, if so, *what* does it report, if not a minimal objective fact . . . to be analysed in terms of sense data?
>
> Let me next call attention to the fact that the experience of having something look **sleazy** to one at a certain time is, insofar as it is an experience, obviously very much like that of seeing something to be **sleazy**, insofar as the latter is an experience. But the latter, of course, is not *just* an experience. And this is the heart of the matter. For to say that a certain experience is a *seeing that* something is the case, is to do more than describe that experience. It is to characterize it as, so to speak, making an assertion or claim and—which is the point I wish to stress—to *endorse* that claim.[19]

Or with *inappropriate* pasted in. Look, there you go:

> Let me begin by noting that there certainly seems to be something to the idea that the sentence 'This looks **inappropriate** to me now' has a reporting role. Indeed, it would seem to be essentially a report. But, if so, *what* does it report, if not a minimal objective fact . . . to be analysed in terms of sense data?
>
> Let me next call attention to the fact that the experience of having something look **inappropriate** to one at a certain time is, insofar as it is an experience, obviously very much like that of seeing something to be **inappropriate**, insofar as the latter is an experience. But the latter, of course, is not *just* an experience. And this is the heart of the matter. For to say that a certain experience is a *seeing that* something is the case, is to do more than describe that experience. It is to characterize it as, so to speak, making an assertion or claim and—which is the point I wish to stress—to *endorse* that claim.[20]

Finally let's see what *unlawful* looks like on the screen share:

---

18. Wilfrid Sellars, *Empiricism and the Philosophy of Mind* (Cambridge, MA: Harvard University Press), 1997), 39.
19. Wilfrid Sellars, *Empiricism and the Philosophy of Mind* (Cambridge, MA: Harvard University Press, 1997), 39. Slightly modified as above.
20. Wilfrid Sellars, *Empiricism and the Philosophy of Mind* (Cambridge, MA: Harvard University Press, 1997), 39. Slightly modified as above.

Let me begin by noting that there certainly seems to be something to the idea that the sentence 'This looks **unlawful** to me now' has a reporting role. Indeed, it would seem to be essentially a report. But, if so, *what* does it report, if not a minimal objective fact . . . to be analysed in terms of sense data?

Let me next call attention to the fact that the experience of having something look **unlawful** to one at a certain time is, insofar as it is an experience, obviously very much like that of seeing something to be **unlawful**, insofar as the latter is an experience. But the latter, of course, is not *just* an experience. And this is the heart of the matter. For to say that a certain experience is a *seeing that* something is the case, is to do more than describe that experience. It is to characterize it as, so to speak, making an assertion or claim and—which is the point I wish to stress—to *endorse* that claim'.[21]

Mrs P. 'That's actually quite clever, yes I see what you are getting at, at least I think I do. So, terms like "sleazy", "unlawful", and "inappropriate" can all sit in a possible relation to one another and we can endorse them if we see them in the right justificatory relationships, operating coherently in a particular "language-game" or whatever. So, in a particular, let's call it, "feminist language-game" we can infer from "sleazy" something "inappropriate" or even "unlawful". Though, I know this is probably too Wittgensteinian a way to put it. I realize Sellars uses different words, but can't remember off the top of my head: something about the "spaces of reason" or . . .'

KAP. 'Sorry to cut across you, but he actually does use Wittgensteinian terminology at certain points in the book. But, yes, you're nearly right, the more famous phrase is "the logical space of reasons", of, as he says, "justifying and being able to justify what one says". As punishment for getting the phrasing wrong, I'm going to quote the actual passage—last one I promise—where he uses these very words. From reading around, this is probably the most often cited passage I've come across (probably why you were able to approximate it off the top of your head). It is in section 36. Sellars writes:

'The point I wish to make . . . is . . . that one couldn't have observational knowledge of *any* fact unless one knew many *other* things as well. And let me emphasize that the point is not taken care of by distinguishing between *knowing how* and *knowing that*, and admitting that observational knowledge requires a lot of 'know how'. For the point is specifically that observational knowledge of any particular fact . . . presupposes that one knows general facts of the form X *is*

---

21. Wilfrid Sellars, *Empiricism and the Philosophy of Mind* (Cambridge, MA: Harvard University Press, 1997), 39. Slightly modified as above.

a reliable symptom of Y. And to admit this requires an abandonment of the traditional empiricist idea that observational knowledge 'stands on its own feet'.'[22]

KAP. 'Skipping down a bit further, he then makes the crucial claim:

'The essential point is that in characterizing an episode or a state as that of *knowing*, we are not giving an empirical description of that episode or state; we are placing it in the logical space of reasons, of justifying and being able to justify what one says.'[23]

I know this might sound really odd, but reading Sellars over the last few days has helped me clarify why I had sometimes felt like a bit of a dick for having a go at my mum and her supposed lack of basic feminist sense or credentials. Coming away from those exchanges with Mum at the time, I tended to calibrate them in terms of the obvious historical, hermeneutical, and generational distance that separated us. But beyond this vague kind of Gadamerian resignation to the inevitability of prejudice . . .'

Mrs P. 'Wha, who?'

KAP. 'Hans Georg Gadamer, the guy who wrote *Truth and Method* and who famously argued against the "prejudice against prejudice", who influenced a generation of major political theorists when we were coming up in the 90s . . .'[24]

Mrs P. 'The fusion of horizons guy?'

KAP. 'Yes, that's the one! I guess the cereal box version of such a "fusion of horizons" would be my Mum and I having a more sympathetic understanding of each other's interpretive "life-world" as experienced here and there, there and then. This is gesturing towards the idea of an "effective historical consciousness", to butcher one of Gadamer's other well-known phrases. What I'm wondering is whether Sellars could possibly add something else into the mix here?'

Mrs P. 'What do you mean? What does Sellars give you that a Gadamerian hermeneutics doesn't?'

KAP. 'I don't really know how precisely to frame this yet, but it is something like a process sociology of knowledge with some political intent'.

Mrs P. 'Oooh, fancy . . .'

---

22. Wilfrid Sellars, *Empiricism and the Philosophy of Mind* (Cambridge, MA: Harvard University Press, 1997), 75–76.

23. Wilfrid Sellars, *Empiricism and the Philosophy of Mind* (Cambridge, MA: Harvard University Press, 1997), 76.

24. Hans Georg Gadamer, *Truth and Method* (London: Continuum, 2005). I'd imagine Kerry-Ann is referring to political theorists like Charles Taylor here. See, for example, Charles Taylor, *Sources of the Self* (Cambridge, MA: Harvard University Press, 1992).

KAP. 'Piss off, will you! Look, help me to think of it this way. The problem with a kind of cereal box Gadamerian hermeneutics is its lack of sociological traction and emancipatory intent'.

Mrs P. 'Is this like a Habermasian thing? Like when he talks about "emancipatory knowledge interest" in *Knowledge and Human Interests*?'

KAP. 'Yes, I suppose it could be, now you mention it. You know I'm getting more and more into Habermas in my old age. I didn't know you were into Habermas?'

Mrs P. 'There's a lot you don't know about me, girlfriend!'

KAP. 'Really?'

Mrs Ps. 'No, not really!' [laughs]

KAP. 'You. Are. Hilarious! Anyway, with apologies to Habermas, the sociology of knowledge I am thinking about here would be the kind of qualitative work done in various organizational settings where you would basically look at the processes of meaning making, knowledge making, the credentialising of particular norms, values, and activities within the said corporate setting'.[25]

Mrs P. 'An organizational or corporate setting like a university, for instance?'

KAP. [laughs] 'Funny you should mention that! Let me cut to the chase with my hunch. So, rather than explaining away the things we might call "prejudice", "abuse", "sleaziness", "inappropriate", or even "unlawful behaviour" as always interpretive gestures that must acknowledge and relativize "wrongdoing" as a necessary and unavoidable epiphenomenal consequence of time and place ("well that's what it was like back then, Kerry-Ann"), you do something else. You take the thing you are looking at (whether it's systematically prejudicial and patriarchal employment law, the sexually abusive antics of some bastard on a 1960s factory-floor, or the sleazy and inappropriate gestures of a male professor in 90s academia) and you say it's not simply a matter of hermeneutical interpretation "all the way down". You take the thing that you are looking at and determine it as "wrongdoing" by locating it in a "logical space of reasons". You basically connect it to a justificatory process, the to and fro of argumentation and political contestation. You communicatively or linguistically establish connections between residual cultures and activities once described as "banter" and justifiably assert that there are good reasons to reconceptualize and transfigure them into clearly discernible forms of "sleaziness", "inappropriate", and/or "unlawful behaviour" or whatever'.

---

25. Interestingly, this echoes some of the sociological literature that 'Laing' implicitly referred to in his interview with Kerry-Ann, Iain, and Robert in part 1.

Mrs P. 'So how is that different to Gadamer's "fusion of horizons", or even Habermas's notion of "communicative rationality" for that matter? Aren't they all part of the same "linguistic turn"? I know they may well be turning in slightly different ways and directions, but the turns are all linguistic. Doesn't this kind of "linguistification of the sacred"—to steal a rather nice phrase from Habermas—not fall prey to the kind of relativist concerns you just articulated?[26] Isn't there a kind of sociological reduction of "observation reports" to the context of their linguistic articulation? Doesn't the emancipatory intent then lose important purchase and potentially fly off into frictionless abstraction, to the bureaucratic netherworld; the "he said, she said" of organizational complaint that never goes anywhere and changes precisely nothing? I mean we've all been there. You hardly need me to remind you what I went through on that score? Now I'm beginning to appreciate your Mum's realpolitik and pragmatic attitude to the 60s factory floor she had to negotiate! Perhaps a little more hermeneutical savvy would have been better for me looking back on my own experiences. Yes, I was coming up decades behind your mum, but maybe I could have benefitted from her hard-earned wisdom? Now that I think of it, you were absolutely right when you made the explicit connection between your Mum's experience and ours. Yes, you were definitely right: the distance is anything but intergalactic. It's all very local . . .'

KAP. 'That's a thought that really stings, really hurts, really makes me angry! A thought that really is going to fester. Look, to bring it back to Sellars, you may well be right that there is nothing but a cigarette paper between him and the likes of Gadamer and Habermas. But I have to confess I find Sellars "naturalism" intriguing in this context. Again, I'm no expert, but from what I have read, it seems like the most influential interpreters of Sellars—obviously, Rorty, but also guys like McDowell and Brandom—have tended to emphasize the linguistic side and maybe play down his "naturalism".[27] Now, by "naturalism" here I simply mean that there is some causal—if "causal" is the right word—connection between the work of justification that is mediated through language and undertaken in a "logic space of reasons" AND something like the raw feel or experience of seeing something one might

---

26. The notion of a 'linguistification of the sacred' is one of Habermas's most famous phrases. The phrasing suggests that we move beyond some collective sense of awe or fear in the face of an unknowable transcendence and toward a situation in which the norms we live by are a product of an all-too-human endeavour: 'communicative action oriented to mutual understanding', a 'post-metaphysical' lifeworld in which 'the force of the better argument' guides a 'rational reconstruction of society'. See Jürgen Habermas, *The Theory of Communicative Action* (Cambridge: Polity Press, 1986). Also, see Jürgen Habermas, *Post-Metaphysical Thinking* (Cambridge: Polity Press, 1995).

27. See, for example, Robert Brandom, *From Empiricism to Expressivism: Brandom Reads Sellars* (Cambridge, MA: Harvard University Press, 2015); John McDowell, *Having a World in View: Essays on Kant, Hegel, and Sellars* (Cambridge, MA: Harvard University Press, 2013).

later construe or assert as, say, "wrongdoing", or "inappropriate", or "unlawful behaviour", or as "sleaziness", or what have you. I mean Sellars couldn't be any clearer in *Empiricism and the Philosophy of Mind* that sense data, a see-ing *that* (*that* his hand is there, *that* the law systematically discriminates, *that* the solidarity of the union guys clearly doesn't extend to female colleagues) implies something is happening, events, raw feels, or experiences in the order of "being". Of course, yes, we can't "know" anything about *that* happening, event, raw feel, or experience unless and until we mediate our understanding of it through language and assert it in the "logical space of reasons". But in maintaining a distinction between "being" as a kind prelinguistic grasping, apprehension, attention, and/or openness to the world and the linguistically mediated knowledge of what it is we are grasping, apprehending, attending, or being open to is precisely what is intriguing for me. I wonder whether in that space in between "being and being known" (to steal yet another famous phrase from Sellars) something interesting is happening?[28] I wonder whether this something *happening* can connect back to my idea of a kind of process sociology of knowledge with emancipatory intent?'

Mrs P. 'My head hurts. I'm supposed to be the philosopher here lecturing you. You realize what is really *happening* here?'

KAP. 'What?'

Mrs P. 'You've contracted the disease! Stop reading Sellars and grow up! Get yourself a good Rortian therapist!'

KAP. [laughs]

---

28. A passing reference to Wilfrid Sellars, 'Being and Being Known', Proceedings of the American Catholic Philosophical Association 34 (1960): 28–49.

~

PART FOUR

The Class on 'Space Traders'

I don't much like being in my office on campus, but was glad that I happened to be there on the day one of my colleagues happened upon me in a bit of a state; 'Robert, I can't believe these students, but they won't let up on me. They're on my back again about using the "Space Traders" story in class'. It was very disturbing to see my colleague in such a state. Even though he has given me permission to use his name in what follows (and clues or a trail of crumbs leading to his real identity are evident below at various points for those of you who are particularly curious), I thought I would call him Professor Golightly (Professor G henceforth), as this is the name of the key character of the story in question. Professor G was some twenty-six years my senior, a brilliant, committed, and intellectually daring scholar whose work I knew, and respected, long before I was lucky enough to be his colleague. Professor G is an eminent social scientist, a sociologist, a grounded theorist, a symbolic interactionist in the tradition of George Herbert Mead. Never one to shy away from looking at difficult social issues, never one to obsessively worry about slipping on an intellectual or political banana skin, never one to play the petty political organizational and institutional games of craven academic self-promotion, never one to compromise on his philosophy of education in the increasingly marketized edu-factory that is the contemporary academy, I always looked up to Professor G. This was why I found it so difficult to see him in such a state, seemingly so scared and upset by the 'upset' he supposedly caused.

Some context is needed here. The story of 'The Space Traders' is a science fiction parable that comes at the end (chapter 9) of Derrick Bell's brilliantly provocative masterwork: *Faces at the Bottom of the Well: The Permanence of Racism*. If you'll forgive me, I'd like to quote some fragments of the first few paragraphs of the text to illustrate the crucial, jaw-dropping conceit of the story. Bell begins with his 'three surprises':

1 January

The first surprise was not their arrival. The radio messages had begun weeks before, announcing that one thousand ships from a star out in space would land on 1 January 2000, in harbours along the Atlantic coast from Cape Cod to North Carolina. Well before dawn on the day, millions of people across North America had wakened that day to witness the moment the ships entered Earth's atmosphere. However expected, to the watchers, children of the electronic age, the spaceships' approach was as awesome as had been that earlier one of three small ships, one October over five hundred years before, to the Indians of the island of Santo Domingo in the Caribbean.

No, the first surprise was the ships themselves. The people . . . saw . . . huge vessels, the size of aircraft carriers . . .

As the sun rose on that bright cold morning, the people on the shore, including an anxious delegation of government officials and media reporters, witnessed a fantastic display of eerie lights and strange sound—evidently the visitors' salute to their American hosts. Almost unnoticed during the spectacle, the bow of the leading ship slowly lowered. A sizable party of the visitors—the first beings from outer space anyone on Earth had ever seen—emerged and began moving majestically across the water toward shore. The shock of seeing these beings, real in appearance and bearing, literally walking on the waves was more thrilling than frightening . . .

Then came the second surprise. The leaders of this vast Armada could speak English. Moreover, they spoke in the familiar comforting tones of former President Reagan, having dubbed his recorded voice into a computerized language-translation system.

After the initial greetings, the leader of the U.S. delegation opened his mouth to read his welcoming speech . . . But before he could begin, the principal spokesperson for the space people (and it wasn't possible to know whether it was a man or woman or something else entirely) raised a hand and spoke crisply, and to the point.

And this point constituted the third surprise. Those mammoth vessels carried within their holds treasure of which the United States was in most desperate need; gold, to bail out the almost bankrupt federal, state, and local governments; special chemicals capable of unpolluting the environment, which was becoming daily more toxic, and restoring it to the pristine state it had been before Western explorers set foot on it; and a totally safe nuclear engine and fuel, to relieve the nation's all but depleted supply of fossil fuel. In return, the visitors wanted only one thing—and that was to take back to their home star all the African Americans who lived in the United States.[1]

Three surprises then. The huge vessels carrying the alien space traders, their computationally pitch perfect Reaganite English, their jaw-dropping proposition; give us your African Americans and we'll deliver you from an economic and ecological crisis. Intellectual and political gelignite!

Professor G had a long-standing interest in Derrick Bell, both his life and work. For those of you who do not know, Bell was a lawyer by training, a civil rights activist and latterly a law professor. After nearly ten years of practicing law, Bell moved into academia, distinguishing himself as the first African American professor of law at Harvard in the early 1970s. Famously, in the early 1990s, his tenure at Harvard ended in protest at the lack of diversity of tenured faculty.[2] Contrasted with Bell's earlier and more overtly 'systematic' or 'scholarly' legal writings—a book like, say, *Race, Racism and American Law*[3]—*Faces at the Bottom of the Well* seemed to hold a special allure for Professor G. Before becoming a sociologist, Professor G studied law, and he never lost an interest in interpreting the everyday machinations of legal systems and practices (what he called, drawing somewhat creatively on Thomas Kuhn, 'normal legal practices') in sociological terms. Those of you who know Professor G's work will no doubt recognize this in his 1999 book, *Towards a Process Sociology of Everyday Legal Practices*. Understanding the everyday rough and tumble of legal practice as a 'social world' in which meanings are processed, contested, solidified, challenged, etc., Professor G often drew on Bell and what he described as the latter's 'sociological imagination and method'. This, as some of you may already know, refers to the method of 'provocative auto-ethnographic dramaturgy'. Professor G first coined this phrase in the mid-1990s, citing Bell's *Faces* as his main influence and inspiration. If I have understood the notion properly, or at least simply put, 'provocative auto-ethnographic dramaturgy' is a method that draws down into day-to-day, first-person experiences in order to craft stories and create dramatizations, imagined scenarios, that provoke readers to see the social world differently. The provocation, then, is twofold. The first (perhaps

---

1. Derrick Bell, *Faces at the Bottom of the Well: The Permanence of Racism* (New York: Basic Books, 1993), 158–60.

2. That is to say, in 1990 Derrick Bell took an unpaid leave of absence from Harvard to protest the fact that not a single African American woman served on the law faculty. As we will discuss below, this 1990 protest became something of a national political issue or controversy in the United States some twenty-two years later during Barack Obama's presidential campaign in 2012.

3. Derrick Bell, *Race, Racism, and American Law* (Boston: Little, Brown, 1973).

more political provocation) is the suggestion that this kind of approach can have real concrete resonance and relevance in the social field; namely, that it does the job of provoking readers to interpret their lifeworld in a new way, shaping their actions accordingly. Relatedly, the second (perhaps more methodological provocation) is the idea that different forms of storytelling, various ways of dramatizing sociopolitical life, or that the work of the imagination more generally, can, in principle, yield something of real sociological and epistemological import; namely, in making or provoking us to know the social world differently.[4]

I don't want to rehearse in detail Professor G's provocations or arguments in this context. The reader can go off and look at his *Towards a Process Sociology of Everyday Legal Practices* if she or he wants to. Let us simply proceed with the idea that Bell's *Faces* neatly illustrates and exemplifies the method Professor G refers to as 'provocative auto-ethnographic dramaturgy'. In his preface to the book, Bell himself refers to the 'unorthodox form' of its argumentation, pointing out that 'several of the stories were written to facilitate classroom discussion'. Interestingly, and on more than one occasion, Professor G described *Faces* to me as a kind of cross between J. L. Austin's *How to Do Things with Words* and Deleuze and Guattari's *A Thousand Plateaus*. When I asked him what he meant by that (and I asked him more than once), he'd go off on another one of his weird tangents and I could never get him back on point. I mention this because I think the connection here is something to do with all three texts being born in the classroom, or being the product of exchanges with students and others, or part of a broader collective assemblage of articulation, something irreducible in its polyvocal expression. We know that *How to Do Things with Words* was a lecture series pulled together by students and published after Austin died. Perish then publish! See what I did there?[5] We also know *A Thousand Plateaus* as that dizzyingly transdisciplinary text, a number of years in the collective making, a product of an ongoing research seminar with input from various folk from a range of different subject specialisms.[6] And we know

---

4. To get a sense of some of the sociological literature that may well have been influencing Professor G at this time, see Anna Banks and Stephen Banks, eds., *Fiction and Social Research* (London: Rowman & Littlefield, 1998).

5. Apparently, Austin was very reluctant to publish during his lifetime, thinking that it was rather vulgar, even cravenly ambitious, to publicly disseminate scholarly work with such abandon. That this might seem utterly perverse to subsequent generations of scholars clearly shows how in thrall we are to the academic publishing industry. We academics seem to increasingly think of scholarly output as naturally part of a broader, supposedly, 'creative', economy. A point well made some time ago by Chris Gibson and Natasha Klocker, 'Academic Publishing as "Creative" Industry, and Recent Discourses of "Creative Economies": Some Critical Reflections', *Area: Royal Geographical Society* 36, no. 4 (2004): 423–34.

6. A point well made by Ian Buchanan, *Assemblage Theory and Method* (London: Bloomsbury, 2020).

that Bell clearly played out the dramas that make up the text of *Faces* (not just his science fiction story 'The Space Traders', but various other imagined scenarios and dialogical exchanges with a varying cast of characters) for his students on an ongoing basis. You can see this in the poly-subjective flow of the writing, in the clamouring contestation of any number of different voices in *Faces*. You can also see it in the gritty, polyvocal vernacular of language-games specifically chosen to further the story, language-games that would otherwise potentially spin off into abstraction where Bell not quite such a skilled writer and communicator. In this regard, the 'Space Traders' story is exemplary. At first glance, the conceit of the story seems the stuff of fairly banal, overly didactic, crudely fantastical science fiction. But what is brilliant about the form in which the story unfolds is its 'realism', as it were. By 'realism' I mean something like a realpolitik sensibility that anchors the text as a totality and draws the reader in. Most immediately, there is 'realism' in the sense of the kind of 'legal realism' and 'racial realism' that Bell's scholarly work is rightly taken to exemplify. In a well-known article that he published in the *Connecticut Law Review*, Bell describes the critical force of 'legal realism' in the following terms:

> The Realists' critique suggested that the whole liberal worldview of private rights and public sovereignty mediated by the rule of law needed to be exploded. The Realists argued that a worldview premised upon the public and private spheres is an attractive mirage that masks the reality of economic and political power. This . . . attack had profoundly threatening consequences: it carried with it the potential collapse of legal liberalism. Realism, in short, changed the face of American jurisprudence by exposing the result-oriented, value-laden nature of legal decision making.[7]

As we see, for Bell, an overly formal 'legal liberalism' that 'masks economic and political power' helps to explain the 'result-oriented, value-laden nature of legal decision making'. Perhaps the best example of this for Bell—and certainly the most well-known—is the 1954 Supreme Court decision on racial desegregation: *Brown versus Board of Education*. Bell has very little truck with liberal-progressivist forms of talk when it comes to *Brown*. As far as Bell is concerned, the liberal-progressivist story about mid-twentieth-century racial desegregation in the United States will remain simplistically naïve for as long as we fail to account for the real historical, cultural, economic, and political forces that actually influence legal decision making. In the case of *Brown*, Bell emphasizes the significance of the Cold War, seeing the movement on

---

7. Derrick Bell, 'Racial Realism', *Connecticut Law Review* 24, no. 2 (1992): 368.

racial desegregation very much as a response to the Soviet's characterization of mid-twentieth-century US capitalism as a racially structured economic system. Put crudely, for Bell, racial desegregation in mid-twentieth-century United States was little more than geopolitical, Cold War public relations. As Bell often emphasized, legal instruments or formal legal calls for racial desegregation were nothing new in US political history, in fact they were around one hundred years old by the time of the Brown decision. So, what explains the timing of *Brown*? Why didn't this kind of law find its way into the statute book in the 1850s or 1890s or 1910s or 1930s, rather than the 1950s? In his 1980 *Harvard Law Review* article, 'Brown versus Board of Education and the Interest-Convergence Dilemma', Bell gives us his answer. Put simply, it's a legal-realist or racial-realist argument that says the law of the United States changes 'for the better'—whatever 'for the better' might mean—when it is in the interests of the dominant white class, when the interests of marginalized, oppressed, or subjugated groups converge with majoritarian white interest.[8] In the case of *Brown*, to repeat, a key factor was the propaganda or PR war with the Soviet Union, the convergent necessity of countering the Soviet's damning accusation that the history of American capitalism is irreducibly and structurally stained by racism and the subjugation of indigenous and/or colonized peoples. This, of course, had immediate geopolitical significance in the developing world at the time, particularly if we think about it in relation to the rise of 'African Nationalism' and the USSR's strategic support of the same. Bell puts it like this:

> I contend that the decision in *Brown* to break with the Court's long-held position on these issues cannot be understood without some consideration of the decision's value to whites, not simply those concerned about the immorality of racial inequality, but also those whites in policymaking positions able to see the economic and political advances at home and abroad that would follow abandonment of segregation. [For instance,] . . . the decision helped to provide immediate credibility to America's struggle with Communist countries to win the hearts and minds of emerging third world peoples.[9]

Leaving these broader geopolitical and historical considerations aside, perhaps the best way of dramatizing the concept of 'interest-convergence' is to hand the narrative baton over to Bell as it is brilliantly depicted by him in the 3 January entry of the 'Space Traders' story. Here we find the real Profes-

---

8. Derrick Bell, 'Brown versus Board of Education and the Interest-Convergence Dilemma', *Harvard Law Review* 93, no. 3 (1980): 518–33.
9. Derrick Bell, 'Brown versus Board of Education and the Interest-Convergence Dilemma', *Harvard Law Review*, 93, no. 3 (1980): 524.

sor Gleason Golightly addressing the hastily formed 'Anti-Trade Coalition', a group of black and liberal white politicians, civil rights representatives, and progressive academics who have quickly come together to oppose the Trade. This group, Bell tells us, work feverishly in developing an oppositional strategy. Bills challenging the Trade were drafted for Congress, plans for direct action protests were drawn up, there were even discussions of possible large-scale civil disobedience, should the unthinkable 'African-American kidnapping plot', as they called it, get majority support in the proposed referendum. Just as those in the meeting are about to settle on their plans of action and resistance, Golightly prevails upon the 'Anti-Trade Coalition' to propose an alternative proposition, what we could call the 'interest-convergence' proposition or strategy. Now, as Bell points out, Golightly, ever the realpolitik careerist, often exhibited the ability to step very lightly and skilfully when it came to his negotiation of the politics of race. His connection with a conservative administration and active support of its racially discriminating policies naturally make him a figure of suspicion in the black community. Suspicious or not of his motives, the 'Anti-Trade Coalition' grant Golightly the platform for a few brief minutes. Bell describes the scene in the following detail:

As he moved toward the podium, there was a wave of hostile murmuring whose justification Golightly acknowledged: "I am well aware that political and ideological differences have for several years sustained a wide chasm between us. But . . . events . . . have transformed our disputes into a painful reminder of our shared status. I am here because, whatever our ideological differences . . . , we all know that black rights, black interests, black property, even black lives are expendable whenever their sacrifice will further or sustain white needs or preferences."

Hearing Golightly admitting to truths that he had long denied, served to silence the murmuring. "It has become an unwritten tradition in this country for whites to sacrifice our rights to further their own interests. This . . . overshadows the debate about the Space Traders' offer and may well foretell our reply to it . . .

"I realize that our white liberal friends continue to reassure us. 'This is America', they tell us. 'It can't happen here'. But I've noticed that those whites who are most vigorous in their assurances are least able to rebut the contrary teaching of historical fact and the present reality. Outside civil rights gatherings like this, the masses of black people—those you claim to represent but to whom you seldom listen—are mostly resigned to the nation's acceptance of the Space Traders' offer. For them, liberal optimism is smothered by their life experience.

"Black people know for a fact what you, their leaders, fear to face. Black people know your plans for legislation, litigation, and protest cannot prevail . . . Indeed, your efforts will simply add a veneer of face-saving uncertainty to a debate whose outcome is not only predictable, but inevitable . . ."

"Professor Golightly," the chairman interrupted, "the time we have allotted you has almost expired. The delegates here are weary and anxious to return to their homes so that they can assist their families through the crisis. The defence plans we have formulated are our best effort. Sir, if you have a better way, let us hear it now."

Golightly nodded. "I promised to be brief, and I will . . . The question is how to best counter an offer that about a third of the voters would support even if the Space Traders offered America nothing at all. Another third might vacil-late, but we . . . know that in the end they will simply not be able to pass up a good deal. The only way we can deflect, and perhaps reverse, a process that is virtually certain to result in approval of the Space Traders' offer, is to give up the oppositional stance you are about to adopt, and forthrightly urge the country to accept the Space Traders' offer."

He paused, looking out over the sea of faces. Then there was a clamour of outraged cries: "Sell out!" "Traitor!" and "Ultimate Uncle Tom!" The chair-man banged his gavel in an effort to restore order.

Seemingly unmoved by the outburst, Golightly waited until the audience quietened, then continued. "A major, perhaps the principal, motivation for racism in this country is the deeply held belief that black people should not have anything that white people don't have. Not only do whites insist on better jobs, higher incomes, better schools, but they also usurp our culture . . . Whites exploit not only our music but our dance, language patterns, dress and hairstyles as well. Even the badge of our inferior status, our color, is not sacro-sanct, whites spending billions a year to emulate our skin tones . . . So whites' appropriation of what is ours and their general acquisitiveness are facts—facts that we must make work for us. Rather than resisting the Space Traders' offer, let us circulate widely the rumour that the Space Traders, aware of our long fruitless struggle on this planet, are arranging to transport us to a land of milk and honey—a virtual paradise . . .

"Although you are planning to litigate against the Trade on the grounds that it is illegal discrimination to limit it to black people, mark my words, our 'milk and honey' story will inspire whites to institute such litigation on the grounds that limiting the Space Traders' offer to black people is unconstitu-tional discrimination against whites!

"Many of you have charged that I have become expert at manipulating white people for personal gain. Although profit has not in fact motivated my actions, I certainly have learned to understand how whites think on racial is-sues. On that knowledge, I am willing to wage my survival and that of my fam-ily. I urge you to do the same. This strategy is, however risky, our only hope."

The murmurs had subsided into stony silence by the time Golightly left the podium.[10]

---

10. Derrick Bell, *Faces at the Bottom of the Well: The Permanence of Racism* (New York: Basic Books, 1993), 174–76.

Let us leave Bell's Professor Golightly there (though you may well have guessed or indeed know that things will not end well for him and his comrades in the 'Anti-Trade Coalition' . . .) and come back to our own Professor G. In the last couple of years Professor G and I had developed a close relationship, partly driven by the fact that we have been working together on a book, a joint-authored monograph that we are having lots of fun talking about, but not quite getting to down to write with any great urgency, at least not yet. Although, I should say the fun we have had talking about it is explained, to some degree, by the intellectual conceit and form of the book project itself. The book we are working on is a dialogue, and the register of it, the conversational ebb and flow of it, we are seeking to capture as a live, lively, and, even at times, rather associative exchange of ideas and arguments. The best way to do this, or so we reasoned, was through a regular (usually weekly) online meeting that we would record and then transcribe, before working it up into a text that was accessible and readable to a broad, fairly popular, audience. What is reproduced below (and only slightly edited and cleaned up by me) is a meeting we had about a week after Professor G burst into my office to tell me that some of the students were again on his back about the content of his teaching. Like a lot of our meetings, this one veers off topic. Actually, it never gets to the topic, as we never get down to talking about our own book project.

Robert Porter (RP). 'Look, before we start discussing the book I just wanted to say that I'm sorry I had to cut things a little short in the office last week. I'm sorry we didn't have a chance to talk properly . . .'

Professor G (PG). 'I really wasn't in the head space to say anything very useful or coherent anyway. So, please, don't worry! By the way, how did it go with the paper you were writing for this conference coming up. What's it on again?'

RP. 'Oof, I don't know! The conference is on "Universities, Critique, and Neoliberalism". The usual "critical university studies" nonsense. I head off tomorrow, if I can actually be bothered to travel . . .'

PG. [laughs] 'Appropriate, though, eh? A little too close to the knuckle after last week methinks . . .'

RP. 'Indeed! Anyway, are you OK now? Are you feeling a bit calmer? Can you maybe tell me better what happened last week?'

PG. 'Well, after the session the week before last, I was naturally feeling a bit nervous. So, I thought what I'd do was show the *Space Traders* film to the particular seminar group with the disruptive ones in'.

RP. 'Oh yes, the weekly Tuesday 12.15 "pop alt-right" crowd you were telling me about?'

PG. 'That's the one . . .'

RP. 'Wait, what, there's a *Space Traders* film? Like a documentary or something? Maybe a piece on the whole hullabaloo concerning Bell and Obama sparked by *Breitbart* and *Fox* during his campaign to get re-elected President in 2012?'[11]

PG. 'No, I'm referring to an actual fictional piece made for HBO. It went out in the mid-1990s as part of a series or anthology called *Cosmic Slop*, a reference to the *Funkadelic* album. George Clinton even hosts the HBO show. It was kind of like a *Twilight Zone* thing. Robert Guillaume played Professor Gleason Golightly'.[12]

RP. 'Who is Robert Guillaume when he's at home?'

PG. 'You're probably a bit too young to remember the American show from the late 1970s, *Soap*. But he was the butler, "Benson".'

RP. 'Yes, yes, I vaguely remember a young Billy Crystal in that. There was a spin-off show too, wasn't there?'

PG. 'Exactly. It was called *Benson!*'

RP. [laughs] 'Strange that! It's coming back to me now, Benson the sardonic butler, and the show, *Soap*, a parody of the daytime soaps of the day. OK, yes. Anyway, getting off track here, so HBO made a version of Bell's story that went out in the mid-90s? Wow, all I thought HBO did before shows like *The Sopranos* and *The Wire* appeared was pay-per-view sports, boxing in particular.[13] You live and you learn; if only I'd been at your 12.15 seminar!'

---

11. In 1990, Derrick Bell, at that point still teaching at Harvard, took an unpaid leave of absence to protest the fact that not a single African American woman served on the law faculty there. His protest was sparked, in large part, by Harvard's failure to grant tenure to Regina Austin, a very well-qualified African American woman. The students supported Bell in his protest and held a rally as a show of that support. At one demonstration, a young Barack Obama introduced Bell to his audience of fellow law students by urging them to: 'Open up your hearts and minds to the words of Professor Derrick Bell'. This was latched on to by *Breitbart* and *Fox* in Spring 2012 as video of Obama's speech appeared and was then used in an (ultimately failed) attempt to derail his re-election campaign.

12. The creative force behind the path-breaking *Funkadelic-Parliament* music collective, George Clinton et al. released *Cosmic Slop* in 1973, their fifth studio album. Created by Rod Serling in the late 1950s, *The Twilight Zone* was to become one of the most well-known franchises in US popular culture. For an interesting philosophical survey of the cultural significance of this show, see Nöel Carroll and Lester H. Hunt, eds., *Philosophy in The Twilight Zone* (Oxford: Blackwell, 2009).

13. For a discussion of the historical impact of HBO on screen and popular culture, see, for example, see Dean Defino, *The HBO Effect* (London: Bloomsbury, 2014). Better still, see Victoria

PG. 'I wish you had been there! As I said, given the general direction and tone of the previous sessions, I decided to try to keep the conversation to a minimum and fill up the hour with an introduction and screening of *Space Traders*'.

RP. 'Remind me again? What was it that happened the week before last?'

PG. 'Well, it actually started in the first week of the semester. You know the way I do a lecture on "critical theory and the academy" in week one?'

RP. 'Yes. Is that where you do the stuff on how the Cold War shaped the postwar American academy? By the way, I've started dipping into that book you recommended on how the Cold War impacted folk like Carnap, Frank, Neurath—essentially depoliticizing the type of logical empiricism they brought over to the US in the mid-twentieth-century. That book has been playing on my mind a fair bit recently'.

PG. 'You mean George Reisch's *How the Cold War Transformed the Philosophy of Science*? Great book that, the subtitle is the kicker—"*To the Icy Slopes of Logic*". I'm not normally into detailed cultural history or archival work, but Reisch is brilliant in showing this journey to the icy slopes of a supposedly depoliticized logic. You see, and it's not talked about enough, the political vitality of logical empiricism and Otto Neurath's Unity of Science movement was quashed almost as soon as it arrived on US shores by a Cold War anticommunism at play both within the academy and beyond (for instance, external agents like Hoover's FBI were particularly active in the academic space). That's to say, Reisch painstakingly shows how this Cold War anticommunism begins to shape the curricula of the mid-twentieth-century US academy and even how it influenced the research of its leading philosophers of science'.[14]

RP. 'So what are you trying to do here? I think I know . . .'

PG. 'Well, sorry to interrupt, it's clearly a not so subtle nod to the history of, what we now journalistically call, the "culture wars" in the US academy'.

RP. 'Are you baiting these alt-right kids, Professor G?'

PG. 'This is the thing, Bobby: I genuinely had no idea that some of the students (granted a very small minority) were reading what we are rather journalistically calling "alt-right" stuff on the internet. I got a bit of an inkling in week one, as I said there a moment ago. But, THEN, in the week-two lecture I happened in passing to refer to Adorno as a well-known and

McCollum and Giuliana Monteverde, eds., *HBO's Original Voices: Race, Gender, Sexuality, and Power* (London: Routledge, 2019).

14. George Reisch, *How the Cold War Transformed the Philosophy of Science: To the Icy Slopes of Logic* (Cambridge: Cambridge University Press, 2010).

leading figure in the "Frankfurt School Critical Theory" and an influential "cultural Marxist".'[15]

RP. 'Yeah, you can't even use that term anymore?'

PG. 'Cultural Marxist?'

RP. 'Yes!'

PG. 'But, I don't understand: why? All I was saying was the usual, pretty banal, thing about the Frankfurt School's Marxist focus on culture and what we used to call "mass media", and how this is an important departure from a classically Marxist focus on relations of production blah blah blah . . .'

RP. 'Jesus, what planet have you been living on?'

PG. 'Huh?'

RP. 'You should read the work of someone like Alan Finlayson. He's a political theorist at University of East Anglia, a cultural-political theorist I'd say, who has done some interesting work on how concepts like "cultural Marxist" get baked in the furnaces of populist right-wing online spaces only then to find their way into more "mainstream" forms of political discourse. I mean think about a term like "woke". It's everywhere!'[16]

PG. 'Oh, gosh, yes, I seem to vaguely remember a Tory politician re-cently use the term "cultural Marxist" and a bit of fuss was made of it'.

RP. 'Yes, it was a woman called Braverman I think, a junior Brexit min-ister at the time. You know where the term comes from, or at least her lazy usage of it?'[17]

PG. 'No?'

RP. 'Remember Anders Breivik?'

PG. 'That neo-Nazi guy who went on a murder spree in Norway?'

RP. 'That's the one!'

PG. 'Christ, I've just Googled it here, you're right'.

RP. 'What have you Googled?'

PG. 'A story from The Guardian has come up. This junior Tory minister Braverman, you're right, was giving a speech in March 2019 to a Euro-sceptic think-tank (by the way, why are all think-tanks nutty and right-wing???) called the Bruges Group. This is what she said according to the report:

---

15. For an excellent historical survey of the Frankfurt School of Critical Theory made famous by Adorno and his equally famous comrades in 'The Institute of Social Research', see Martin Jay, *The Dialectical Imagination: A History of the Frankfurt School* (Berkeley: University of California Press, 1973).

16. See, for example, Alan Finlayson, 'Neoliberalism, the Alt-Right, and the Intellectual Dark Web', *Theory, Culture, Society* 38, no. 6 (2021): 167–90.

17. It is quite funny that in Spring 2022 Robert only had a vague idea of the woman who would become UK prime minister only three years later. Such are the slings and arrows of political fortune.

We are engaging in many battles right now . . . [We] . . . are engaged in a battle against cultural Marxism, where banning things is becoming de rigueur; where freedom of speech is becoming a taboo; where our universities, quintessential institutions of liberalism, are being shrouded in censorship and a culture of no-platforming.'

RP. 'Notice the targeting of us, "we", the woke cultural Marxists of the universities . . .'

PG. 'Wait, there's more. She continues:

We have culture evolving from the far left which has allowed the snuffing out of freedom of speech, freedom of thought. No one can get offended any more, we are living in a culture where we are putting everyone in cotton wool, a risk-averse mentality is now taking over.

'And more of the same shit:

And that instinct for freedom, for risk-taking, for making mistakes, for innovation, for creativity, is being killed. And it's absolutely damaging for our spirit as British people, and our genius, whether it's for innovation and science, or culture and civilisation . . . .'[18]

RP. 'Hilarious! Well, not so hilarious actually . . .'

PG. 'Granted things are not as bad here in UK universities as they are in the US, but the State mission creep is real enough, isn't it? I feel like such an idiot, Bobby, I really do . . .'

RP. 'Why?'

PG. 'Well, on the one hand, I'm only too well aware of the history and politics of the "culture wars" in the US context (shit I've been teaching it a long time, thinking about Cold War politics and the university for years, thinking about the "critical race theory" of folk like Bell, etc). Yet, on the other hand, I'm utterly shocked when it washes up on our shores. You thought I was taking the piss out of the alt-right kids in my class? No, not a bit of it. I wasn't baiting them. They were certainly baiting me though.'

RP. 'Are you going to tell me what actually happened?'

PG. 'They keep accusing me of promoting what they call "leftist bias", of trying to indoctrinate them and poison their minds with lefty conspiracy

---

18. All of these quotes would seem to be taken from the following article published in the *Guardian* on Tuesday 26 March 2019: 'Tory MP Criticised for Using Anti-Semitic Term "Cultural Marxism".' You can find this on the *Guardian* online archive at: https://www.theguardian.com/news/2019/mar/26/tory-mp-criticised-for-using-antisemitic-term-cultural-marxism.

theories, of being against freedom of thought. One of them is particularly bright and is very good at turning my own words against me . . .'

RP. 'What do you mean?'

PG. 'Well, in one of the classes, I was talking about the—broadly Kantian—idea of "enlightenment" and I couched it in basic terms as a kind of maturity and confidence that can come with trusting yourself, trusting in your critical faculties, trusting in your ability to think for yourself, you know . . . not accepting things at face value, challenging the dogmas of tradition and so on. This, then, gets thrown back in my face (rather skilfully it has to be said) as I get accused of infantilizing the students by dulling their critical faculties, telling them what to think and forbidding them to challenge the lefty dogmas and prejudices that I'm constantly bringing into classroom . . .'

RP. 'So you would be interrupted mid-flow, in the middle of class?'

PG. 'Yes, constant interruptions . . .'

RP. 'The arrogance and the cheek . . .'

PG. 'No, hang on, this is the clever thing about it. The interruptions were never caustic or rude. In fact, they always had the air of being perfectly reasonable in the context of our discussions . . .'

RP. 'Perfectly reasonable? I'm not sure I follow you? I can't imagine these alt-right kids engaging in a critique that was anything other than arrogant and caustic'.

PG. 'You're an admirer of Roland Barthes, aren't you?'

RP. 'What? I don't follow, but yes, I am . . .'

PG. 'There's a bit in Mythologies, a section, I think it's something like "Blind Critique" or something . . .'

RP. [laughs] 'I'm laughing because I was reading Mythologies just the other day. The section or short chapter is entitled "Blind and Dumb Criticism", I think'.

PG. 'So you have a copy of it in your office there?'

RP. 'Mythologies?'

PG. 'Yes'.

RP. 'Yes, it's actually here, at the bottom of that pile of books on my desk'.

PG. 'Grab it there. I have my copy here, too . . .'

RP. 'Hold on, ok, let's see —yes, I was right, it's "Blind and Dumb Criticism". It's the first, second, third, fourth, FIFTH section in the text'.

PG. 'OK, let's have a look. Yes, this is it, this is what I was thinking of. Great, I can just read it to you directly to make my point? Read along with me, if you like'. [laughs]

RP. 'Whenever you're ready, boss, I've got all the time in the world . . .'

PG. 'Cheeky upstart. OK, Barthes writes (and I quote):

Critics (of books or drama) often use two rather singular arguments. The first consists in suddenly deciding that the true subject of criticism is ineffable, and criticism, as a consequence, unnecessary. The other, which also reappears periodically, consists in confessing that one is too stupid, too unenlightened to understand a book reputedly philosophical. A play by Henri Lefebvre on Kierkegaard has thus provoked in our best critics . . . a pretended fear of imbecility (the aim of which was obviously to discredit Lefebvre by relegating him to the ridicule of pure intellectualism).

Why do critics thus periodically proclaim their helplessness or their lack of understanding? It is certainly not out of modesty: no one is at more ease than one critic confessing that he understands nothing about existentialism; no one more ironic and therefore more self-assured than another admitting shamefacedly that he does not have the luck to be initiated into the philosophy of the Extraordinary; and no one more soldier-like than a third pleading for poetic ineffability.

All this means in fact that one believes oneself to have such sureness of intelligence that acknowledging an inability to understand calls into question the clarity of the author and not that of one's own mind. One mimics silliness in order to make the public protest in one's favour, and carry it along advantageously from complicity in helplessness to complicity in intelligence . . .'[19]

PG. 'Bear with me, I'm also going to read a bit of the concluding paragraphs of the section in question'.

RP. 'You go, boyfriend!'

PG. [laughs] 'Alright, OK, be quiet. So, Barthes concludes:

To be a critic by profession and to proclaim that one understands nothing about existentialism or Marxism (for as it happens, it is these two philosophies particularly that one confesses to be unable to understand) is to elevate one's blindness or dumbness to a universal rule of perception, and to reject from the world Marxism and existentialism: "I don't understand, therefore you are idiots."

But if one fears or despises so much the philosophical foundations of a book, and if one demands so insistently the right to understand nothing on the subject, why become a critic? To understand, to enlighten, that is your profession, isn't it? You can of course judge philosophy according to "common sense"; the trouble is while "common sense" and "feeling" understand nothing about philosophy, philosophy, on the other hand, understands them perfectly. You don't explain philosophers, but *they* explain you. You don't want to understand the play by Lefebvre the Marxist, but you can be sure that Lefebvre the Marxist understands your comprehension perfectly well, and above all (for I

---

19. Roland Barthes, *Mythologies* (New York: Noonday Press, 1972), 33.

believe you to be more wily than lacking in culture) the delightfully "harmless" confession you make of it'.[20]

RP. 'So what are you saying? These students are trying to come off reasonable by pretending they don't understand you while sticking the knife in?'

PG. 'Yes, that's part of it. There's definitely that thing that Barthes mentions; that is, "I don't understand what you're saying to me, therefore you are idiotic". But, in a way, they have more subtlety than that. It is all to do with the register they use . . .'

RP. 'Register? You mean in the sociolinguistic sense . . .'

PG. 'Maybe, yeah, that's a good way of thinking about it, actually. But what I was thinking of more particularly relates to the notions of "common sense" and "feeling" that we just read off Barthes. I think it has something to do with the *subjective register* of *my* "common sense" and "feelings"; the me, myself, and I . . .'

RP. 'I'm not sure if I'm following you here . . .'

PG. 'OK, in the first class I do on "critical race theory" I begin with the two seemingly contradictory propositions and I say both of them are "true" in their own way. Proposition 1: "there is no such thing as race". Proposition 2: "racism is a permanent social fact". As you can probably guess, I try to draw on the literature—Bell, of course, but also Crenshaw, and, closer to home, folk like Stuart Hall and Paul Gilroy—to try to wrestle with the implications of the "truth" of these propositions.[21] Proposition 1 is used to open up a broadly theoretical or philosophical discussion about race that moves us away from thinking about race as thing-like, something approximating a ready to hand object. Simply, you can't talk about race in the way you talk about electrons, telephones, cheese, bins, notebooks, garden fences, nectarines, and so on. To even begin to talk about "race", to make it an object of your discursive concern, you must acknowledge that such talk is anchored in sociopolitical life; in routines of identification, in modes of subjective experiences, in institutional-political power relations, in generic representations, in everyday organizational or work-life, in a specific kind of media ecology and so on.

Proposition 2 is meant to open up the discussion more sociologically, to look at the seeming permanence of racism as a social fact, when both looked

---

20. Roland Barthes, *Mythologies* (New York: Noonday Press, 1972), 34.

21. See, for example, Kimberlé Crenshaw et al., *Critical Race Theory* (London: The New Press, 1996); Kimberlé Crenshaw et al., *Seeing Race Again: Countering Colorblindness Across the Disciples* (Oakland: University of California Press, 2019); Stuart Hall, *Selected Writings on Race and Difference* (Durham, NC: Duke University Press, 2021); Paul Gilroy, *There Ain't No Black in the Union Jack* (London: Routledge, 1987); Paul Gilroy, *The Black Atlantic* (London: Verso, 1993).

at historically and in a contemporary context. So, racism seems to be a permanent social fact in the way, say, historically speaking, poverty does, or class inequality, or gender inequality. That is to say, whether we like or not (though, clearly, we shouldn't like it), history and sociology teach us that just as the poor will always be with us, so too will these other forms of class, gender, and race-based inequality. Now, the conceit of running these two propositions together is to capture a kind of mixed quality of emotions that comes with: a) thinking or hoping (channelling proposition 1) that if there is no such thing as "race" other than that shaped by social and political life, then surely we can shape sociopolitical life better to challenge and call out racism when and where we see it; b) while recognizing (channelling proposition 2) that the persistence of racism as a social fact is something we should despair of, remain realistic about, be angry and impatient about, but desire to critique and change with real and enduring tenacity . . .'

RP. 'Oof, not an easy thing to do when you're a privately educated upper-middle-class white guy from the suburbs . . .' [laughs]

PG. 'You're laughing, but that's too true, and these alt-right kids know it . . .'

RP. 'You mean they're using your own background against you? What? You're some guilt-ridden, "woke liberal do-gooder" or something?'

PG. 'Yeah, this is something I do try to address in class. For there is a certain truth to it, that's why it's not just a joke, that's why they can latch on it. Let's face it: I'm an old, privately educated, upper-middle-class, English white guy from the leafy suburb of Edgbaston. My pedagogical strategy, if I have one, is to acknowledge this at the outset. But then, as I say, I try to bring the students with me to gesture toward the mixed quality of emotions I mentioned a moment ago. I try to do this by aiming to bring to life propositions 1 and 2 and subsequently a) and b) through a discussion of the life and fiction of the great American novelist James Baldwin.[22] Basically, the narrative is this. Step one, whatever your background, whatever your class, gender or racial privilege, you can recognize the truth of propositions one and two. Step two, recognizing the truth of propositions one and two can then lead us to consider the mixed quality of emotions as designated by a) and b). Step three, a) and b)—namely the mixed quality of emotions where hope mixes with despair, where a desire for change mixes with historical and sociological realism about the persistent social fact of racism—is precisely the kind of discombobulating subjective experience brought to life and dramatized

---

22. For a biographical portrait of Baldwin, see David Leeming, *James Baldwin: A Biography* (New York: Skyhorse Publishing, 2015).

so well in Baldwin's fiction.[23] Baldwin is hopeful and in despair at the same time, angrily philosophizing with a hammer against the racism he encounters in his everyday life while simultaneously being historically and sociologically realistic and pessimistic about race relations in his country of birth'.

RP. 'OK, it's a kind of liberal-humanist thing where the power of the novel in illuminating the inner experience of the other brings us into an encounter, exchange, or conversation that has the potential to transform us, to make us think differently? So, while you might be a privately educated, upper-middle-class white guy from the suburbs of Birmingham, this does not mean that a writer with the urgency and brilliance of Baldwin can't give you something approximating a sense of his subjective experience as a mid-twentieth-century African American. That seems a long way from the pessimism of Derrick Bell, no?'

PG. 'Well I don't know about that, Bobby. Bell is a pessimist, for sure, but he is also a brilliant writer, an engaging writer, a writer that can also provoke his readers to think differently about race, about law, and the very idea of justice or whatever else. True, there's not the same love in his heart or on his sleeve, the same fragility and sense of hope against all hope that you get in Baldwin, but there is a stark, striking, and, above all, *tenacious* and *enduring* critique of what I'm calling here the persistent social fact of racism. This is inspiring in its own way I think. Anyway, what you're calling a kind of liberal humanism is all I have to offer here. If there are problems with it, if there are tensions in it, if I'm nothing more than an upper-middle-class English twit or liberal do-gooder, then so be it. Better that than an alt-right ideologue . . .'

RP. 'Hard to argue with you there! But, tell me again, how are your 12.15 alt-right "ideologues" arguing against you? Sorry if I am repeating myself, but I just want to be clear in my head. What actually are they doing?'

PG. 'A bunch of different things. As I've said, they are interrupting me in class constantly. Trying to hoist me up on my own intellectual petard; nicely, though, with a smile and faked bewilderment. So, for instance, in the critical race theory class, they constantly, but always politely, interrupt, suggesting that they are confused and don't understand how there can be no such thing as race while claiming racism is a persistently present social and historical fact. It would tend to go something like this: "Excuse me Professor G, I'm confused. How can racism be challenged if it is a permanent thing?" "Aren't you implicitly saying that there is actually no point in trying to challenge and critique it because racism, like the poor, will always be with us?" "How does

---

23. See, for instance, James Baldwin, *Giovanni's Room* (London: Penguin, 1957); James Baldwin, *Another Country* (London: Penguin, 1963); James Baldwin, *The Fire Next Time* (London: Penguin, 1964).

that then fit with the idea that there is such thing as race?" "For if there is no such thing as race, then there can't be any racism, can there?" "I'm not sure what you mean when you say these things". "I mean I feel it is a really strange thing to say that I'm not a white person?" "But, if you're right, and I'm no particular race at all, then how does that relate to this thing of 'white privilege' that you said you had as a white person and, presumably, the white privilege I have as a white person?" "I mean I feel that I am white. I feel like if I walked down the street and stopped the first person I met and told them that I'm not white, that actually there is no such thing as racial things like whiteness, they'd think I was crazy, that I lost all common sense, no?" "I know that you can't mean all these things, but I just feel utterly bewildered and confused by what you just saying". "Maybe it's just me, I'm sure it is". "Can you maybe explain it again?"'

RP. 'I'm guessing that there is an extra-discursive, gestural pantomime simultaneously being played out during this tirade of questioning'.

PG. 'Exactly, this is where the "blind and dumb criticism" that Barthes talks about assumes a life of its own, as it were. Typically, what happens during these moments is a constant fall back onto "feelings' and 'common sense", but, as you say, via a kind of pantomime performance. Everyone in the class knows, of course, the questions are impertinent, that my authority is being challenged, that they are taking the piss out of me. There is, if not explicit or obvious pantomime villainy, then certainly there is a really hammed up and un-ignorable pantomime comedy, a comedy which is, of course, anything but merely humorous. The exaggerated gestures that accompany the "harmless" (to again use Barthes' lingo) questions—scratching of the head, cocking the head to look like an innocent puppy dog, the eye movement and horizon scanning to draw others in the class into their mischievous eye-line—are all part of an attempted comic seduction that is immediately political. Essentially, what the "harmless" questions and the pantomime comedy are inviting the other students to agree with is a proposition something like this: "Well, isn't it obvious that this old woke liberal do-gooder is funny, ridiculous, and, most importantly, an idiot peddling a weird ideology that actually connects nowhere to everyday experience and common sense"'.

RP. 'So there is never any explicit vitriol or openly aggressive behaviour then?'

PG. 'Sometimes it borders on that in class, there's certainly lots of passive-aggressive behaviour, obviously, but no not really. Outside of class, though, is a different matter . . .'

RP. 'What do you mean?'

PG. 'I've been made aware, and have actually seen, a bunch of stuff on-line. The online activity really kicked off the first time in class I mentioned Bell's "Space Traders" story. You know the bit where Golightly tries to convince the antitreaty meeting to accept rather than oppose the trade, that is, where Bell dramatizes what he elsewhere calls "the interest-convergence dilemma"? You know what that is, don't you?'

RP. 'Yep, basically that we should remain critical and sceptical about overly progressivist liberal narratives regarding the capacity of the law to face down what you've been calling the persistent social fact of racism. Does that sound right to you?'

PG. 'Yes, it does! Now, the twist the 12.15 alt-right kids put on it was that I was teaching "extremist" and "illiberal" ideology . . .'

RP. 'What? Wait, I thought you were a woke liberal do-gooder?'

PG. 'I am! Think about the argument here. It is precisely because that I'm a liberal woke do-gooder that I ended up being seduced by "extremist", "illiberal", "freedom-hating", "racist" ideology . . .'

RP. 'Racist??!'

PG. 'Yes, of course! The narrative goes something like this: the liberal woke do-gooder is so thoroughly and completely seduced by an ideology like "critical race theory"—in their online spaces they actually call it "critical race extremism" or "critical race ideology'—that they remain blinkered regarding its "illiberal", "freedom-hating", and "racist" implications. For, so the argument goes, if we even entertain Bell's suggestion that racism is a permanent thing, or in our terms a persistent social fact, if we accept Bell's claim that so-called liberal progressive legal remedies achieve little and only ever actually come about historically when they converge or dovetail with the interests of dominant white economic and political elites, then you are basically peddling a racialist ideology that condemns us to an eternal war of all against all. In this sense, liberalism, particularly in its more "extremist" and "communist" terms ("extremism" and "communism" are pretty much used interchangeably here), ends up constantly tripping itself up by paradoxically opening the door to a kind of "freedom-hating" "illiberalism"'.

RP. 'So this is why the "Space Traders" story is so provocative for them, right? Because it dramatizes this "interest-convergence dilemma" so starkly?'

PG. 'Yes, exactly!'

RP. 'Holy shit . . .'

PG. 'Another element of their attack, and the thing that has me most worried, why I'm in a such a state at the moment, is that they are also trying to play the consumer-student card against me, threatening complaints both to the senior management here at our place as well as to the office of students nationally'.

RP. 'It's actually called the office for students . . .'

PG. 'OK, whatever the hell it's called! So, in various online spaces, we have direct attacks on me (and, yes, they explicitly name me and all the bad things I'm supposedly doing) alongside, or contextualized in relation to, the liberal sprinkling of text from the office for students, posts or screen grabs from the office for students' independent regulator or whatever that is. All carefully montaged to more than create the impression that there is this woke liberal do-gooder—i.e., me—peddling an illiberal, extremist racial ideology that is deeply distressing for them'.

RP. 'Just googled it while you were talking there. It's the "office of the independent adjudicator" who deals with complaints on behalf of the office for students'.

PG. 'That's the one. In addition, there's a carefully orchestrated campaign internally, the lobbying of other students at our place (student and course reps, the local branch of the students' union, etc.). Here they again adopt the consumer language of the contemporary corporate university, talk about how impoverished their "student experience" is, how they didn't sign up to pay huge fees to have some self-righteous prick of a lecturer use up precious class time to preach at them and try to brainwash them, and so on . . .'[24]

RP. 'A proper double-pincher movement'.

PG. 'Indeed!'

RP. 'But why you? Why have they gone after you in such a deliberate and calculated way?'

PG. 'I brought it on myself a bit . . .'

RP. 'Nonsense! How?'

PG. 'Well, let me take you back to the "cultural Marxism" thing I mentioned before. As we have discovered during the course of our conversation here, I failed to read the room, or didn't understand where this attack on "cultural Marxism" was coming from. Earlier you were asking whether I was baiting them and I said no. But, now that I think of it, maybe I was, without fully realizing it. As I said earlier, I do feel a bit stupid for not realising that some of the US-style "culture wars" stuff would eventually wash up on our shores. I guess if I had the energy to do the kind of work that you mentioned earlier by that UEA guy . . .'

RP. 'Alan Finlayson?'

---

24. This, of course, refers to the time when UK students still paid significant fees for their university courses. Obviously, we now know that that particular economic model imploded and finally collapsed in 2028. What is now emerging from the rubble is a much slimmed down, but publicly funded, higher education sector that is already beginning to feel a lot different to the one experienced by Robert and Professor G in the early 2020s.

PG. 'Yes, that's him, Alan Finlayson! Maybe then I would have seen it coming. Maybe I would have seen how notions like "cultural Marxism" and "interest-convergence" were being reheated in what you called those "alt-right" online furnaces? Maybe I could have dealt with it better, or framed it better?'

RP. 'Are you not forgetting the lesson from Barthes that you were trying to impress upon me?'

PG. 'Huh?'

RP. 'Isn't part of the problem that we often find ourselves immediately trying to respond to "blind and dumb criticism", the kind of criticism that revels in its own desire not to understand—to malevolently, deliberately, wilfully misunderstand, actually—while at the same time demanding to be understood in its own narcissistic and perverse terms. Institutionally, the cards seem stacked against us. For whether we think about pernicious national developments in broad terms of State mission creep (say, our lovely office for students) or more locally about the need for universities like ours to be seen to be providing a consumer-focused "student experience" in a competitive marketplace, the gesture is the same, or our position is the same . . .'

PG. 'Our position?'

RP. 'Yeah, we need to constantly and immediately understand and somehow be sympathetic to those who simply, even wilfully, refuse to understand what we are trying to do'.

PG. 'Oof, that you put it that way. Yes. blind and dumb criticism is hardly equivalent to seeing no evil and hearing no evil'.

RP. 'Just because it sometimes looks like we are constantly encountering stupid or mischievous monkeys throwing shit around shouldn't necessarily blind us to the enduring "problem of evil"'. [laughs]

PG. 'So you're saying that there is no sign of an omnipotent, omnibenevolent, and omniscient God to save us?'

RP. 'Well, if there is, I'm hoping the good Lord will help me out a bit at this upcoming conference. Speaking of which, look, I need to think some more about this paper or "provocation" I'm doing.

Can we chat about the book next week when I get back from Paris?'

PG. '*Perdant!*'

RP. 'Pardon?' [laughs]

PG. [laughs and give two fingers]

~

PART FIVE

The Conference Paper on 'Universities and Critique in a Neoliberal Age'

The conversation with Professor G about 'Space Traders' happened to happen on the day I was supposed to write a paper for an upcoming conference. My plan was to sneak in and spend a couple of hours writing the short paper without anyone noticing I was around. I couldn't work from home that day (working from home is always my preferred choice when I'm writing), so sneak in I did. The paper wasn't really a paper, but a short provocation in which I had a whole twelve minutes to say something about the theme of the gathering: namely, 'Universities and Critique in a Neoliberal Age'. I was simultaneously attracted and repulsed in equal measure by the prospect of doing this twelve-minute provocation. My repulsion you will undoubtedly get a strong sense of as we proceed. Let me say something more immediately about my attraction. I was attracted for a few reasons. First, it would discipline me to do more of the reading I had been doing in the subfield or discipline of 'critical university studies'. Obviously, this would be useful in the context of doing the book with Kerry-Ann and Iain. Second, it would give me an opportunity to actually meet some of the scholars working in this field. Third, and I'm not beyond admitting this, it would provide an opportunity to have a bit of a go at some of the academics who are currently trading on the brand of 'critical university studies'; trading on it in ways that are breathtakingly hypocritical and, quite frankly, disgusting.[1]

---

1. Annoyingly, Robert never makes explicit who the hypocrites are here. But, and as already stated in one of the footnotes in the introduction, if you were interested in sampling some of the more 'critical' takes on the 'neoliberal' university that were out and circulating back when Robert was writing, you could look at the following: Lawrence Busch, *Knowledge for Sale: The Neoliberal*

Before I say something more specific about this hypocrisy, I should say that there are a lot of good people, smart people, doing fantastic work that you could clearly shelter under the scholarly umbrella of 'critical university studies'. I am thinking, for instance, of the kind of qualitatively rich sociological work that really does give the reader a feel for the grit and the grain of the everyday organizational life of the university. For example, I've been recently reading Les Back's quite wonderful *Academic Diary*, a paradigmatic or exemplary book in this regard. Also, I very much admire the kind of 'critical management studies' work that emanated from a certain anarchist strain of thinking at University of Leicester, or recent cultural histories of the organization like Craig Robertson's *The Filing Cabinet: A Vertical History of Information*, or the scholarship of someone like Martin Parker, the author of wonderfully titled books such as *Shut Down the Business School* and *Against Management: Organization in the Age of Managerialism*.[2]

Takeover of Higher Education (Cambridge, MA: MIT Press, 2017); John Smyth, *The Toxic University: Zombie Leadership, Academic Rock Stars and Neoliberal Ideology* (London: Palgrave-Macmillan, 2017); Sinead Murphy, *Zombie University: Thinking Under Control* (London: Repeater Books, 2017); Thomas Docherty, *The New Treason of the Intellectuals: Can the University Survive?* (Manchester: Manchester University Press, 2018); Michael Bailey and Des Freedman, eds., *The Assault on Universities: A Manifesto of Resistance* (London: Pluto, 2011); Stefan Collini, *Speaking of Universities* (London: Verso, 2017).

2. In August 2020 Martin Parker published an article, 'The Critical Business School and the University', in the journal *Critical Sociology*. He asked, 'Can a school of critical management studies survive in the context of a marketizing university that relies heavily on business education for its income?' It turned out that Parker was talking specifically about the anarchist crowd at the School of Business at the University of Leicester. Parker explains in a subsequent one-pager or 'coda' the following year in *Critical Sociology* why he revealed the identity of the 'Provincial University' anonymously named in the original article. Parker writes:

> The 'Critical Business School and the University' was published online in August 2020 . . . Six months after the paper went online, the management at 'Provincial University' made further anonymisation impossible by deciding to 'disinvest' from 'Critical Management Studies' and 'Political Economy'. The paper I published told the story of the School of Business at the University of Leicester, in the East Midlands of England . . .
> As part of a process described as 'shaping for excellence', sixteen members of academic staff at the School of Business were threatened with redundancy at the start of 2021 *because* they taught and researched 'critical' material in an UK business school. They were not identified because of poor teaching or research, or because their courses or modules were set to be closed. It was the fact that they published in journals that had the word 'critical' in their title or worked on topics that were identified as being part of Critical Management Studies or Political Economy that was used as evidence in hearings to make them redundant. Eight of the sixteen were trade union officials. The explicit reason for this 'disinvestment', one supported and articulated by everyone from the Vice Chancellor downwards, was to reshape this School so that it was more relevant to business. At the time of this writing, August 2021, virtually all those academics have now been sacked and many others with critical sympathies have retired or resigned.

See Martin Parker, 'The Critical Business School and the University: A Case Study of Resistance and Co-optation', *Critical Sociology* 47, nos. 7/8 (2020): 1111–24; Martin Parker, 'Coda', *Critical Sociology*, 47, nos. 7/8 (2021): 1125.

All good people! But back to the hypocrites. My disgust or repulsion had two related aspects to it. First, a kind of *spectacular grandstanding*, where the 'critical university studies' academic becomes what Kerry-Ann would call a *big-picture guy* (and yes, all the guys I have in mind here are ALL GUYS) pontificating and gesturing at something real enough ('marketization', 'neo-liberalization', blah blah), but only in a way that maintains their own status and professional prestige. As you will see in the actual paper reproduced below (particularly the few opening paragraphs), I plagiarize the Situationist notion of a 'spectacle of disintegration' and cheekily implicate the hypocritical critics of the university as its passively nihilistic spectators. The second related aspect is something I'm less settled or sure about at this point. But it has something to do with what I would rather roughly call the *currency of scientism in contemporary everyday academic life*. The connections are not nearly clear enough, but if you look at the paper below (particularly the concluding few paragraphs) I begin to gesture toward saying that the very notion of critique apropos the university (and again you can see the influence of Situationism here), is itself critically recuperated by a form of academic capitalism; or, by a kind of capitalist-academic trader trading on a currency I call 'data science'. Some of the supposed 'critics' I have in my tractor beam cynically trade on the 'science' they say they do in order to maintain their professional academic privilege (whether individually within their host institution or apropos other institutions) by way of a competitive individual-ism that stands in a very curious relationship to their professed critique of the 'marketization' or 'neoliberalization' of the university, or their mocking and snarky comments about the vacuity of discourses of 'entrepreneurial-ism' and so on. So, typically, what we get beneath the liberal-lefty sounding critical noises is a competitive individualism that Maggie Thatcher would be proud of. Remember, these guys (ALL GUYS) are Thatcher's children, first generation, as they are all professor-type guys in later middle age. As I write this, I'm reminded of Thatcher's famous dictum about 'economics' being the (scientific?) 'method' that her government had to use to change 'the souls' of the citizenry. Well, it seems to have worked for this generation of soulless and ambitious male professors!

Anyway, hopefully, you will see some of this below. What you will definitely see is a paper that consists of eleven numbered paragraphs. The reason I chose eleven was because it seemed in keeping with the Situationist theme of plagiarism (copying the obvious famous text by Marx on Feuerbach).[3]

---

3. This, of course, is a passing reference to Karl Marx's *eleven* 'Theses on Feuerbach'.

Now, these eleven paragraphs are a bit rough and ready, and you'll see why that is in a moment. But, for now, here they are:

1. To say that the contemporary academy has become a spectacle is to say nothing very much. It's a cliché, a shorthand way of gesturing toward something real enough, objective enough, pressing enough, immediate enough, but not something we want to trouble ourselves with, even though we are necessarily troubled by it. There's a nice joke from Kierkegaard that captures what I'm trying to get at. Kierkegaard writes: 'A fire broke out backstage in a theatre. The clown came out to warn the public; they thought it was a joke and applauded. He repeated it; the acclaim was even greater. I think that's just how the world will come to an end: to general applause from wits who believe it's a joke'.[4]

2. The academic spectacle is a spectacle of disintegration, fire fighting in the absence of any belief that the building is on fire, even when our feet are held to the flames. We engage in a banal exercise fuelled on the thinnest of thin gruel; a supposed sense of humour, a self-regarding irony and a spectatorial detachment that is actually so utterly humourless that we fail to see that the joke is on us. We fail to see that we are knee deep in the same shit as the 'clowns' we mock, despise, and otherwise haughtily look down our noses at. I have used the term 'we' here a few times. The 'we' is we critics, we critical-theoretical scholars, we the academic critics. Or, if that's not bad enough: we the academic critics of the academy. 'Critical University Studies'? Do me a favour!

3. Full disclosure: I'm knee deep in this, working, as I am, on a book on the contemporary university. I'm reading about the emergence and exponential growth of a field of enquiry aiming to 'deconstruct academe', which charts the historical shift away from publicly funded higher education to the much talked about 'neoliberal model', the incessant snarky whining about the 'marketization' of the university by a generation of academics who constantly rolled over, cracked jokes, laughed, who passively, nihilistically watched on as the flames were stoked up by the clowns operating backstage and front of house. The clowns were deadly serious. But oh, how we laughed . . .

---

4. This is a direct quotation from part 1 of Søren Kierkegaard, *Either/Or: A Crumb of Life* (London: Penguin, 2004).

4. Critique atop of critique, cliché atop of cliché, shorthand typing in the face of a blooming buzzing confusion seemingly too blooming confusing to get our heads around. 'Marketization', 'Neoliberalism', 'cheddar cheese with no pickle', so many shorthand phrases, so many clichéd reasons to be less than cheerful.[5] But, of course, we only really provide reasons to be less than cheerful *for show*. Critique in and of the academy almost exclusively comes in a highly cynical, stylized, and mannerist form, like writing a book about the university and already knowing you'll be submitting it for government audit. A culture industry of criticism, where the promise of critique turns out to be little more than the to and fro of academic opinion in a marketplace of ideas. As a currency market, the academic marketplace of critique trades not in a variety of pairs (this and that currency), but in only one pair, at least as far as I can see it. We buy into 'science' and we sell off 'pseudo-science', we value the scientific research that undergirds critique and we devalue the pseudo-scientific impostor or doppelganger. But how can you tell the good twin from the evil twin?

5. The history of critique in the twentieth-century Euro-American academy is a history of war, or at least of the fallout from war. It is a history of the political émigré. Adorno and Horkheimer cashing the US state's cheques during postwar German reconstruction, even after all those nasty things they said about Donald Duck while the war was going on. Marcuse working for the US state department in the fight against 'fascism'. The Logical Empiricists like Frank and Carnap who also went to the United States and who shaped the various 'naturalist' turns in what became the so called 'analytical' philosophy of the latter part of the twentieth-century.[6] In a UK context, think of the Austro-Hungarian origins of Wittgenstein, Feyerabend, Popper, and Lakatos. War, political repression; these things seem to lube the gears of critique.

6. Perhaps after a certain Popperian fashion, Lakatos speaks elegantly, humorously, seriously and somewhat convincingly about the ethico-political stakes that can attend to the 'problem of the demarcation between science and pseudo-science'. As he says:

---

5. This would seem to be a passing reference to an *Ian Dury and the Blockheads* 1979 record 'Reasons to be Cheerful: Part Three'. Apparently, 'Cheddar cheese and pickle' is one of things that Mr Dury and the Blockheads think we should be cheerful about it.

6. It seems Robert wasn't lying to Professor G when he said he was enjoying dipping into the following book: George Reisch, *How the Cold War Transformed the Philosophy of Science: To the Icy Slopes of Logic* (Cambridge: Cambridge University Press, 2010).

The problem of the demarcation between science and pseudo-science has grave implications . . . for the institutionalization of criticism . . . The Central Committee of the Soviet Communist Party in 1949 declared Mendelian genetics pseudo-scientific and had its advocates . . . killed in concentration camps; after . . . Mendelian genetics was rehabilitated; but the Party's right to decide what is science and publishable and what is pseudo-science and punishable was upheld . . . This is why the problem of demarcation between science and pseudo-science is not a pseudo-problem of armchair philosophers: it has grave ethical and political implications.[7]

7. It would seem in very bad taste to even hint at pretending the ethical and political stakes articulated above have anything other than an intergalactically distant connection to the contemporary academy. No doubt that's true! But it doesn't stop me (and call me a self-regarding narcissist if you like) from lamenting the bad taste left in my mouth after years of working in a university, my experience of the kinds people I've had to work for, the line-managers I have been supposedly responsible to. Of course, no-one in university management positions self-identify as 'managers', but as 'leaders'. Clearly, the term 'leader' is easier on the ear, particularly the further you look up the organizational ladder. It seems harder to justify a six-figure salary for a 'manager' when compared to a 'leader'. What does a six-figure salaried university 'leader' look like in practice?[8] A 'happy warrior' who practices what I call (in my more mordant moments, and clearly in bad taste) 'The Pol Pot Strategy of Change Management'. You know the drill: new senior 'leaders' come in and attribute 'bad stuff' to the old or previous regime, promising then the 'good stuff' by way of an organizational 'year zero'. I have seen this happen four or five times now: same shit, different 'leader', same Pol Pot playbook.[9]

8. In addition to the 'happy warrior' persona, in addition to the 'year zero' playbook, I've also noticed a kind of 'Taylorist Scientism' at play in senior university leadership, a 'residual culture' (to steal a phrase from the great Raymond Williams) of 'scientific management' that

---

7. The quote can be found in Imre Lakatos, *The Methodology of Scientific Research Programmes: Philosophical Papers, Vol. 1* (Cambridge: Cambridge University Press, 1978), 6–7.

8. Interesting to read Robert talking matter-of-factly about 'six-figure' salaried 'managers' and 'leaders', particularly from our current historical vantage point. That is to say, we now know, post 2028 crash, how very quickly such salaries became a thing of the past.

9. Attentive readers will undoubtedly note that in using the name 'Pol Pot', Robert is aping the kind of language used by 'Laing' in his *Academic Spectacle*. See part 1. Indeed, we shall see that Robert acknowledges, somewhat regretfully, the connection to 'Laing' below.

now tends to go under the cover of 'data science' or 'data-driven' policy and decision-making. As the history of the organization gets written and rewritten, we can see more and more Taylorist 'scientific management' for what it was/is. An instrument of control, divide and conquer, auditing, monitoring fuelled by a fundamental hatred and mistrust of the 'soldiering' of the 'lazy worker'. It seemed the only 'appropriate' response to early-twentieth-century 'soldiering' was discipline and punishment by way of Taylor's famous stopwatch.[10]

9. Perhaps it is all too easy and predictable to say that in the contemporary university the stopwatch has been replaced by the algorithm, but it's true, in a shitty shorthand or clichéd way. This is our scientism; the scientism of the algorithm is true for our organizational conjuncture (to steal a phrase from the late Louis Althusser). I would argue that data scientism is not only the normative end game for the 'senior leader' in the organizational setting of the university (justifying, as it does, 'evidenced based decision-making'), but that it becomes the endgame across the totality of the institution as such. Within the university we are seeing data scientism increasingly and exclusively becoming the condition of possibility for critique. Critique is the means always relativized to a supposedly, hopefully, data-rich 'impactful' end—'cheddar cheese with extra pickle'. This is as true for the 'critical-theoretical' academic as it is for the 'senior leader'. Sometimes they are one and same person with the same reasons to be cheerful. Such are the 'cultural circuits of capitalism'.[11]

10. You could be forgiven for thinking that I've painted a very negative picture regarding the notion of critique: that critique is, to steal some words from the Frankfurt School, 'conceptually shot through with the logic of the commodity form'. You'd be right! But, of course, I'm only talking about the notion of critique within a very particular domain—the university. Or, more accurately still, I'm only really sharing thoughts of my own everyday experiences in the rough and tumble of the organizational world I operate in. I make no grand

---

10. 'Soldiering' refers to the worker's tactic of working below maximum capacity; what we now are more likely to call 'presenteeism'. This was a particular pet-hate of the father of 'scientific management' Frederick Taylor. As implied, Taylor's response was the 'stopwatch': compartmentalizing tasks on the factory floor and demanding their execution within a strictly specified timeframe. For a good discussion of this, see Gavin Mueller, *Breaking Things at Work: The Luddites Were Right About Why You Hate Your Job* (London: Verso, 2021), 31–36. Also, worth having a look at is a text mentioned explicitly by Robert above: Craig Robertson, *The Filing Cabinet: A Vertical History of Information* (Minneapolis: University of Minnesota Press, 2021).

11. This talk of 'cultural circuits of capitalism' would seem to be a rather cheeky passing reference to Nigel Thrift, *Knowing Capitalism* (London: Sage, 2005).

claims and have no desire to overly generalize or abstract from the above remarks. Such remarks are enough for me in themselves, but, in another way, they are nothing more than a gesture toward what I have taken to calling 'descriptive naturalism'. All I mean by 'descriptive naturalism', at least at this point, is a practice of describing the world in all its absurdity, of believing in the everyday world in all its immediate and discombobulating strangeness. Look at the world, point at it, describe it and through describing it you may well come to know it anew, through the kinds of felt variations that can come with inspecting and articulating its everyday banality in as patient, direct, and non-judgmental a way possible. That takes real work, and, despite appearances perhaps, I'm working on that, believe me . . .

11. The critical-theoretical academics have only transformed the world in a mannerist fashion, the point, however, is to patiently, directly, non-judgmentally describe it in its everyday banality, absurdity, and discombobulating strangeness.

There it is! Warts and all, rough and ready as I said! I've reproduced it pretty much as it was from the handwritten notes I had scribbled on Iain's fancy Japanese notebook the night before the session. I did have another paper on my laptop (a different set of eleven paragraphs, perhaps more carefully crafted than those above), but decided, on Iain's urging, to write a different one, the one you just read. I should explain that Iain and I had gone to the conference together (he was doing a paper, something on Simmel or Goffman about behaviour in public spaces . . .). Anyway, after a chance encounter and a mercifully brief, yet awkwardly tense, conversation at the conference hotel bar with—yes, you've guessed it—one of the *hypocritical big-picture guys*, I started really whining at Iain, complaining about how this guy and his ilk are this, that, and the other thing. Iain, being Iain, listened to my rant (easily ten minutes, probably more) and when I finally ran out of steam, he dipped into his man bag and handed me his fancy notebook and a crappy hotel pen and smiled, saying: 'Why don't you write it up as a rough and ready rant and see how it comes out tomorrow?' That. I. Did. Now, although Iain should not be held responsible or culpable for the shoddiness of my presentation, I do think it is important to suggest that he is, in a way, as much the author of it as I am. It reflects the ongoing conversations we have been having about our own book. Similarly, with Kerry-Ann and my conversations with her about the book, her particular experiences of the particular 'big-picture guys' she has encountered in academia, what she would often frame as the unacknowledged, yet flagrant, contradiction between the 'progressive' or 'comradely' sounding noises made by senior male academics who are simultaneously ruthlessly competitive, individualistic, and not beyond exploiting more junior (more often than not female) colleagues for their own selfish ends. Whether she likes it or not (and she probably wouldn't), Kerry-Ann is very much the author here too.

In the question-and-answer bit of the session one of the hypocrites immediately came after me. Inevitably, he came after me by calling me a hypocrite. The question-cum-series of self-congratulatory statements went along the following lines. First, he quoted/paraphrased a bit of paragraph four back to me, namely: 'Critique in and of the academy almost exclusively comes in a highly cynical, stylized, and mannerist form, like writing a book about the university and already knowing you'll be submitting it for government audit'. Then he asked me this: 'You mentioned in passing that this presentation relates to a book that you and two other colleagues are working on. Isn't that so? So, my question then relates to whether you will be submitting this book for government audit, i.e., submitting to the next REF in 2028 or whenever that is?'[12] Just to be clear: the passive-aggressive charge of hypocrisy directed at me is that I am cynically engaged in state-funded academic production while giving off the surface effect of engaging in a critique of the university. Before I could even try to muster a response to this (on the surface not unreasonable) question, he then made a number of subsequent statements, statements that functioned: a) as a response to what he saw as both implicit and direct criticisms of him in the paper; and b) as an attempt to draw a strong contrast between him as an honest, authentic scholar fighting back against the 'neoliberal' assault on the university and me, the 'effete, mannerist 60s-style Situationist, but without the political commitment of the latter' as he

---

12. Of course, we know now that this conversation about REF was purely academic, that there was no REF2028, that something else happened to the university sector in 2028 that made REF go away. For those of you who don't know, before it was consigned to the dustbin of history, the *Research Excellence Framework* or REF was a pretty big deal in the UK university sector for quite a long time. This can obviously be seen and felt in Robert's narrative and the exchanges he details in the main body of the text. In the end, the main thing that killed REF was the huge cost (hundreds of millions of pounds) of running a massive government audit of academic research by way of peer-review assessment (i.e., academics reading and assessing the 'quality' of the research outputs of their peers). At one point, it was thought that some kind of 'data science' solution would rescue it, that significant savings could be made by using a 'metrics'-based system of assessment amenable to algorithmic or computational calculation. See, for instance, the 2022 article from *The Times Higher Education*: 'Funders Mull Robot Reviewers for Research Excellence Framework'. See https://www.timeshighereducation .com/news/funders-mull-robot-reviewers-research-excellence-framework?fbclid=IwAR1xKj5atiUwK BRtnNFrpnK-xmn763nvr09vHbLTbnyZBVheMR-bWhoweZs. Alas, the robots never delivered . . .

eloquently put it. I have to admit that although I tried to defend myself as robustly as I could, and call him out, I failed. I fluffed my lines and strained to articulate my sincere belief that if there was an effete mannerist critic in the room it was him, not me. Almost as soon as I had finished my strained and faltering response to his pointed question and remarks, I began to regret my lack of composure, cursing myself for my lack of poise, cursing myself that I lacked the cultural or academic capital to spar or trade blows with him.

Smelling blood perhaps, a colleague from the same institution of questioner number 1 (perhaps also seeing himself implicated in what I was doing in the paper) then weighed in with his own series of self-congratulatory statements. Less polished than his more senior colleague, perhaps, but similarly keen to stick the knife. Little did he know, but he would provide me with a second chance to say some of the things that I was already wishing I said to questioner number 1. Questioner number 2 saved me because he serendipitously mentioned Derrick Bell's 'Space Traders' story. He mentioned it in passing, somehow trying to deputize Bell into his argument that the institution and department he worked at were very serious about the business of critique and had foregrounded, blazed a trial for, the study of 'critical race theory' in what he called 'the English-speaking academic world'. Perhaps lacking the eloquence of his more senior departmental colleague, his increasingly crude self-congratulatory remarks, his rather unmeasured, even bombastic, claims about the great things he and his colleagues did and do start to grate a bit on the audience. Sat at the front of the room, questioner number 2 couldn't see the tittering and eye rolling going on behind him. What sealed his fate was his mentioning of REF and how his department was deemed 'one of the best in the world' and 'world leading'.[13] Now, it should be said that he used this phrase ironically, prefacing it with a suggestion that we shouldn't be too obsessed by things like REF, 'After all, it is only a government audit as you say, Robert'.

Mannerism from heaven. 'Then why do you mention it?' I said in response. 'Why is it important for you to school me and the rest of the audience on how great you are?' I continued. Then I went on a rant. I can provide word-for-word detail of this rant because the conference was a hybrid one (both in-person and on Zoom for those who couldn't travel). I should say,

---

13. 'World leading' is a REF term, supposedly the best of the best; research assessed as, quite literally, 'world leading'. In the last REF in 2021, around 36 per cent of all the research assessed was judged as 'world leading'. Now, that over a third of research in the UK was judged as supposedly 'world leading' in 2021 should give some pause for thought, no? Robert once described REF to me as like 'taking part in your kid's school sports day, finishing third in the egg-and-spoon race, and then claiming to be an Olympic-level athlete'. Hyperbolic, perhaps. But, then again, looking at these figures, perhaps not . . .

though, it was quite disconcerting watching the Zoom recording back.[14] I remember feeling full of righteous indignation, feeling very principled in what I was saying, feeling like I was articulating myself as clearly, honestly, and authentically as I could. But when I watch it back (as I've done more than a few times to accurately provide the transcription below) what I primarily see is the very thing I am supposedly criticizing. Here is the rant:

> Then why do you mention it? Why is it important for you to school me and the rest of the audience on how great you are? You say we shouldn't be obsessed with government audits like REF, so why trade on the currency of REF? This is precisely what I was gesturing at in my paper. The character in the paper reflecting on writing a critique of the university then submitting to REF is simply meant as a social commentary that, I'm sad to say, implicates people like you and your departmental colleague who asked the previous question. Let me now answer your colleague's first question a bit more directly now that I've had a chance to think about it: never would I submit a book for publishing anywhere (forgetting REF for a moment) if it wasn't something I thought was truthful and honest. What I think is totally dishonest and cynical is people like you and your colleagues writing books critiquing the marketization of the university while simultaneously engaging in the worst kind of academic capitalism. You guys are proper Thatcherites! Alongside the loud-liberal-lefty progressive noises, there's a barely audible Thatcherite hum, a political philosophy of competitive individualism that you all live by. How else can you explain his [I point at questioner number 1] strategic immersion in things like REF. After all, your esteemed colleague is on a REF subpanel, isn't he?[15] After all, doesn't most of the state money dished out by REF mainly go to institutions like yours, ones that just happen to be in a similar geographical or metropolitan locale? Or do you just trouser that money ironically, or maybe burn it in the Quad, Situationist style. Hey, like *the KLF*?[16] I mean for fuck's sake, who do you think you are kidding, Mr . . .

---

14. Again, for all you younger readers and historical amnesiacs, 'Zoom' was a cloud-based video conferencing service that was very popular in the early 2020s, particularly after the first wave of the Covid-19 pandemic hit.

15. If you have a taste for arcane historical detail or information about how REF subpanels worked in the past, you can blow some of your carbon footprint allowance here: https://www.ref.ac.uk/panels/. Robert's point, of course, is a more political one, concerning the strategic importance of making sure that staff and researchers in your own host institution get a foot in the subpanel door; that is, be part of the everyday decision-making process and assessment in order to ensure the most favourable result possible.

16. A Scottish electronic band that emerged and rose to prominence in the 1980s and 1990s, the *KLF* famously burned one million pounds in a disused boathouse on the island of Jura in August 1994. 'K Foundation Burn a Million Quid' was framed a piece of performance art and video at the time.

The panel chair at this point interrupts and asks me to stop talking. I should indeed stop talking, but, alas, I don't . . .

> Let me just say one more thing! You mention Derrick Bell's 'Space Traders' story and, rather perversely, you seek to use that as part of a narrative about your wonderfulness as an institution. Let me remind you, if I may, about one of key ideas that Bell dramatizes in the story; his provocative notion of 'interest-convergence'. One of the great things about Bell, and in particular a book like *Faces at the Bottom of the Well*, is that he so brilliantly puts us on our guard, makes us rightly sceptical of folk in privileged positions who sound off in 'progressive' ways ONLY when it is in their selfish interests to do so. Your problem is that you guys don't know whether to shit or get off the pot. For example, we have just seen how you champion your REF credentials ironically, as if the irony somehow gets you off the hook, somehow disguises your ethos, the card-carrying political philosophy of competitive individualism (to again butcher a phrase from the great C. B. Macpherson) that you implicitly and, as we have just seen, EXPLICITLY live by!!!¹⁷ If I were you, I'd take the time to reread Bell again before ever deputising him into your 'neoliberal' storytelling. You bang on about 'critical race theory', but it's utterly meaningless grandstanding. It's blah, cheddar cheese and no pickle . . .

Again, the chair interrupts me and this time properly shuts me up. Thankfully! I say 'thankfully' because I find myself utterly embarrassed, even shamed, by the tone of my remarks as I watch them back and transcribe them here. Talk about personifying the smug self-congratulation of the idiot who thinks he is baiting an idiot. I couldn't help but be reminded of books like Laing's *Academic Spectacle* and the conversations with Laing and others that we had when Iain, Kerry-Ann, and I first started kicking around the idea of our own book on the contemporary university. But this is not just about Laing's book, which at least had some interesting drama in it. It's about a way of being an academic, engaging in a mode of critique, the cynicism of academic capitalism more generally, the generic pull of a particularly macho way of defending your position and supposedly taking down 'idiots' with supposedly 'slam dunk' arguments that, in actuality, are little more than diatribe. Looking at my own behaviour here, it was clear that, I, too, had succumbed to a kind of (let's call it Laingian or pop-Situationist) seduction; a particular institutional persona, the mouthy critic that dares to 'speak truth to power' or some such nonsense. It was bullshit, the same bullshit I was supposedly critiquing. Fighting bullshit with bullshit leaves everyone covered in it, blinded

---

17. This would seem to be a passing reference to the classic that is: C. B. Macpherson, *The Political Philosophy of Possessive Individualism: Hobbes to Locke* (Oxford: Oxford University Press, 1962).

by it. As I put it in the presentation, it was mere critique atop of critique, cliché atop of cliché, gestural, anxious, almost animalistic, noises made in the face of a blooming buzzing confusion that simultaneously leaves one both giddy and bereft. But what was making me dizzy? What did I feel I had somehow lost? Speaking philosophically, I suppose, I felt that I had lost my sea legs, that the stuff (was it concrete? water? quicksand?) beneath my feet was moving me around, staggering me into a sickly feeling that any ambition I had of working with Kerry-Ann and Iain to provide something resembling a critique of the university was simply unrealistic and naive, something already recuperated, as it had been, or so I thought, by a form of academic capitalism that seemed to provide its very conditions of emergence. So, not so much a pop-Situationist, more a depressed and nihilistic one.

As you can see, at the end of the presentation (paragraph 10) I try to comfort myself with the thought that even though the very idea of a critique of the university is—to again steal a phrase from the critical theorists of the Frankfurt school—'conceptually shot through with the logic of the commodity form', we can nonetheless engage in something I rather gnomically call 'descriptive naturalism'. To repeat, what I'm gesturing at is a way of describing the world in all its absurdity, of believing in the everyday in all its immediate and discombobulating strangeness. If we look at the world, engage in the ostensive act of pointing at it, if we describe it as patiently, directly, and non-judgmentally as we possibly can, then maybe, just maybe, by describing it in this way we may well come to know it anew. Yet, with that thought, I still felt bereft. Lost to a form of description that, at best, provides nothing more than a trail of crumbs, some clues, the promise of pointing and looking at something that could somehow be transfigured by the very gesture or act of looking and pointing. The promise here, of course, is that description becomes something akin to an aesthetic experience, a new felt sensation, or variety of 'felt variations' as I call them in the presentation above. Could it be that there is a particular art to engaging in 'descriptive naturalism'? Could such an art, when well-practiced, lead us to new ways of knowing the thing thus inspected and then articulated its everydayness? So, methodologically speaking, then, is it a question of trying to make good on the idea that description becomes naturalized when it becomes an art that carefully and patiently attends to the everydayness of the thing depicted?

From: Robert Porter
Sent: 7 July 2022 11:43
To: Porter, Kerry-Ann; MacKenzie, Iain
Subject: The Conference Paper on 'Universities and Critique in a Neoliberal Age'
Hiya,

I've attached some thoughts and reflections on the conference Iain and I attended in May. As you will see from the attached (which also includes the actual script I delivered on the day), I'm feeling a bit like I've lost my way, that maybe all of us have lost the run of things—at least as far as the book is concerned. I was trawling through old emails this morning and I'm left wondering whether we have really progressed things in the way that we thought we should or could. I was particularly struck by our exchanges around the time of the 'Laing' scandal (is 'scandal' the right word?) when you both reassured me that the 'phenomenology' of the contemporary edu-factory that we were motivated to do need not have any of the haughtiness or arrogance or belligerence of Laing's *Academic Spectacle.* You both talked about the importance of doing a no-frills kind of 'phenomenology', suggesting that this simply implied a careful and detailed elucidation of the 'day and daily' of academic-organizational life. In some ways, I think that this is what I am groping at in the attached when I'm using this phrase 'descriptive naturalism'. I guess a big part of what I'm agonizing about in the attached remarks is the status of 'critique' here. You will see that I play around with the (pop-Situationist?) idea that the critique of the university is 'shot through with the logic of the commodity form'—in this case, a kind of 'academic capitalism', 'the political philosophy of a competitive individualism', always-already shaping the institutional persona of the so called 'critical' or 'progressive' academic etc . . .

So, I'm left wondering whether the 'critical' work we think we are doing, the 'critique' of the contemporary edu-factory that we think we are currently engaged in, is nothing much more than an epiphenomenal puff of smoke from a train chugging along regardless, a train that we arrogantly thought we were going to derail. Sorry, really overextending the metaphor.

Anyway, and not for the first time, I ask: am I being a drama queen here? Or, maybe better still, am I raising the stakes too much and expecting too much?
R

From: Iain MacKenzie
Sent: 7 July 2022 14:58
To: Porter, Robert; Porter, Kerry-Ann
Subject: RE: The Conference Paper on 'Universities and Critique in a Neoliberal Age
Drama queen!!!!!

Thought I'd get in there before Kerry-Ann did!

Seriously though, I do think that what you are calling 'descriptive natural-ism' is basically what we have been calling phenomenology. I do wonder, though, about your final sentence. You ask; 'So, methodologically speaking, then, is it a question of trying to make good on the idea that description be-comes naturalized when it becomes an art that carefully and patiently attends to the everydayness of the thing depicted?' Although, I should say, I'm pretty sure that this is what we have been trying to do, each in our way. I mean when I look at the fragments of text that we have been sharing for the book I very much think that we have been 'carefully attending to the thing depicted'. My query, I suppose, concerns why you are invoking the notion of 'naturalism' in this context? It has a rather ambitious and positivistic sound to it, no? As for your worry that any criticisms we may have of the contemporary edu-factory are somehow recuperated, or even conditioned by, the economic-institutional circumstances of their articulation? Well, yes and no! I think recuperation is a two-way street. To say that the contemporary university cynically trades on its supposedly 'critical' and 'progressive' credentials is a fairly banal sociological remark, no? But THAT it does so, gives 'we' scholars within those institutions the space to potentially do 'critical' and 'progressive' things, albeit within certain institutional constraints. I guess what I'm saying is that it is not an absolutist either/or (the ideologically pure critique versus the recuperated and institutionally overdetermined critique). It's always a relativized either/ or, where you are always asserting some autonomy while, at the same time, getting screwed or manipulated a bit. Didn't Kierkegaard say that you were always a bit screwed either way? ☺

Aw'ra,

Iain.

From: Kerry-Ann Porter
Sent: 7 July 2022 17:43
To: Porter, Robert; MacKenzie, Iain
Subject: RE: The Conference Paper on 'Universities and Critique in a Neo-liberal Age'

Hi Iain, Robert,

I wonder whether the notion of 'naturalism' that Robert is playing around with here has any connection to some of things that came up in my discus-sions with 'Mrs Pills' about our PhD days, *Academic World*, etc.? Remember I sent you guys that stuff a while back? To refresh our memories, I was pulling a bit on my rather amateur and (probably) confused engagement with Wilfred Sellars' *Empiricism and the Philosophy of Mind*. Right at the end of our conversation I seem to just flat out confuse my old PhD comrade by talking about 'naturalism' in the context of a relationship between the justification of what we 'know' through language—undertaken in what Sellars famously calls the 'logic space of reasons'—AND its immediate connection to something like the raw feel or experience of something in situ. So, the idea is that the raw feel or experience of something in context implies an event, a happening in the world. Of course, if we want to be Sellarsian about it, we'd have to say that we can't, strictly speaking, 'know' anything about that happening or event unless and until we mediate our understanding of it through language. But, and I think this is what potentially connects back to Robert's 'descriptive natural-ism', in maintaining a distinction between 'being and being known', as Sellars might say, I wonder whether something interesting is happening. Put bluntly, I wonder whether what happens in between 'being and being known' can be thought of as a sociopolitical process, can somehow be connected to the thing I called (with apologies to Habermasians everywhere) a 'process sociology of knowledge with emancipatory intent'. Or, maybe, my old friend and PhD com-rade was right to mock me for entertaining such thoughts . . .

P.S. Robert—maybe I'm overinterpreting your use of the word 'crumbs' toward the end of thing you emailed over? But you say you are worried about being lost 'to a form of description that provides nothing more than a trail of crumbs'. This made me think about Kierkegaard. Iain your implicit reference to *Either/Or* (also referenced, of course, in your original presentation Robert) no doubt also helped to plant the idea. At the minute, I'm actually reading a relatively recent (2009) translation of Kierkegaard's *Repetition* alongside what is usually translated as his *Philosophical Fragments*. Interestingly, though, in this translation, Mr M.G. Piety (I joke not, this is his real name), trans-lates the Danish *Philosophiske Smuler* not as *Philosophical Fragments*, but as *Philosophical Crumbs*. I'm going to leave you both, by cutting and pasting Mr Piety's rationale here:

> The present translation uses 'crumbs' rather than 'fragments' for two reasons. First, there was a Danish cognate of the English 'fragments' in Kierkegaard's time (*Fremmedordbog* . . .) which Kierkegaard could have easily chosen but did not. Second. Kierkegaard may well have chosen *Smuler* over *Fragmenter* (the plural of the Danish *Fragment*) because it alludes to the well-known Danish saying *Smulerne er også Brød* (The crumbs are also bread) which, in turn, al-ludes to Matthew 15: 21–8.[18]

---

18. Mr Piety quoted in Søren Kierkegaard, *Repetition/Philosophical Crumbs* (Oxford: Oxford Uni-versity Press, 2009), 181.

Strange isn't it, the associations and the connections you make when your mind wanders in and out of other minds . . .

Kerry-Ann

From: Robert Porter
Sent: 9 July 2022 17.55
To: Porter, Kerry-Ann; MacKenzie, Iain
Subject: RE: The Conference Paper on 'Universities and Critique in a Neoliberal Age'

Oof, that's really interesting Kerry-Ann! Prompted by your email, I actually had a look at my own copy of *Philosophical Fragments* (mine is obviously an older translation)! I don't know if you came across this bit, it's section 241 in the original. Strangely, it made me feel a lot better about what we are trying to do. Anyway, Kierkegaard writes:

> If someone were to say: 'What you are making up is the shabbiest plagiarism ever produced, in that it is no more nor less than what every child knows', then I would have to shamefacedly hear that I am a liar. But why the shabbiest? Every writer who steals, steals from another writer; thus, we are all equally shabby; my theft is perhaps less harmful in that it is more easily discovered. But who is the author? If I were so polite as to consider you, you who judge me, as the author, you would again become angry. Is there then no author when there is a story? That would be strange, like hearing a flute despite the fact that there was no flute-player. Is this story like a proverb, the author of which is unknown because it is as if the whole human race had written it? Was it perhaps therefore that you called my plagiarism the shabbiest because I did not steal from an individual person, but robbed . . . the whole race?[19]

Stick that in yer pipe and smoke it, Roland and Michel!!![20]

R

From: Robert Porter
Sent: 9 July 2022 19.03
To: Porter, Kerry-Ann; MacKenzie, Iain
Subject: RE: The Conference Paper on 'Universities and Critique in a Neoliberal Age'

Sorry, got carried away with the Kierkegaardian crumbs there and forgot to come back on your points . . .

---

19. Søren Kierkegaard, *Repetition/Philosophical Crumbs* (Oxford: Oxford University Press, 2009), 109.

20. Both Roland (Barthes) and Michel (Foucault) famously problematized the notion of 'authorship' in their work. I'm guessing these are the guys sticking it in their pipe here for Robert.

Let me try to—hopefully briefly—respond to what you guys have been saying.

The use of the term 'naturalism' was maybe a little crummy (see what I did there Iain?). Actually, maybe we could overextend the crummy metaphor without causing it too much injury or muscle damage? Maybe 'descriptive naturalism' is the crumbs, but still the bread too, as it were? Not an over-ambitious positivism, but a modestly detailed elucidation of our encounters and experiences in a particular social world or corporate space—the edu-factory—we love to hate, but only because we love it in the first instance. Does it really matter what we call it? 'Descriptive Naturalism versus Banal Phenomenology?'. Either way, as you say Iain, maybe we gain a little autonomy while getting screwed a bit?

Maybe the Kierkegaardian connection you made there Kerry-Ann interests me precisely because it is the kind of intriguing associative thinking that comes from conversing and writing as a three, rather than as a one? Maybe the fragments of text that we have been working on are so many crumbs that could be rolled together into various doughy shapes? Maybe these associations are that much freer, speculative, and interesting, because, as a three, we avoid a more deadening, self-regarding, stultifying, overbearing, and singular responsibility for the text(s) we have created?

Maybe this talk of a shared creative activity can bring us back round to the notion of 'critique', and particularly the more modest critique you spoke of Iain? A critique, never absolutely pure, but always relative to the situation in which it takes on significance. We know that for Professor G, the sociological and political importance, the critical importance, of a writer like Derrick Bell was brought to life through the method he liked to call 'provocative auto-ethnographic dramaturgy'. Now, 'provocative auto-ethnographic dramaturgy', let us remind ourselves, is again a modest method; one that draws down into everyday, first-person experiences in order to craft stories which provoke readers to see, interpret, and then know their social world differently. This is not quite 'Emancipatory-Knowledge Interest' in the Habermasian sense Kerry-Ann, but that does not mean that it is completely without any critical import or potential transformative power, right?[21]

Thanks guys! No 'maybe' about it, I really was being a drama queen about the critique/recuperation thing. I'm back on board. Let's keep rolling with the crumbs . . .

R

---

21. Seemingly a reference to the Habermasian text mentioned previously in the conversation between Kerry-Ann and Mrs Pills in part 3 above: namely, Jürgen Habermas, *Knowledge and Human Interests* (London: Heinemann, 1981).

From: Kerry-Ann Porter
Sent: 10 July 2022 09:45
To: Porter, Robert; MacKenzie, Iain
Subject: RE: The Conference Paper on 'Universities and Critique in a Neoliberal Age'
Yeah Robert, until your next crisis next week or whatever . . .
DRAMA QUEEN!!!!!!!
Kerry-Ann

From: MacKenzie, Iain
Sent: 10 July 2022 10:41
To: Porter, Kerry-Ann; Porter, Robert
Subject: RE: The Conference Paper on 'Universities and Critique in a Neoliberal Age'
Damn it, too fast for me there Kerry-Ann!
Aw'ra,
Iain

Bibliography

Anderson, Sven, Alan Butler, David Capener, Donal Lally, Clare Lyster, and Fiona McDermott. *States of Entanglement: Data in the Irish Landscape*. Barcelona: Actar Press, 2021.

Back, Les. *Academic Diary*. London: Goldsmiths Press, 2016.

Bailey, Michael, and Des Freedman, eds. *The Assault on Universities: A Manifesto of Resistance*. London: Pluto, 2011.

Baldwin, James. *Another Country*. London: Penguin, 1963.

———. *The Fire Next Time*. London: Penguin, 1964.

———. *Giovanni's Room*. London: Penguin, 1957.

Banks, Anna, and Stephen Banks, eds. *Fiction and Social Research*. London: Rowman & Littlefield, 1998.

Barthes, Roland. *Mythologies*. New York: Noonday Press, 1972.

Bell, Derrick. 'Brown versus Board of Education and the Interest-Convergence Dilemma,' *Harvard Law Review* 93, no. 3 (1980): 518–33.

———. *Faces at the Bottom of the Well: The Permanence of Racism*. New York: Basic Books, 1993.

———. *Race, Racism and American Law*. Boston: Little, Brown, 1973.

———. 'Racial Realism,' *Connecticut Law Review* 24, no. 2 (1992): 363–79.

Benoot, Tiesj. *The Folk-Psychological Implosion of Philosophy of Mind: Toward a Neuroscientific Critique*. Oudenaarde: Flandrian Press, 2029.

Bergson, Henri. *Laughter: An Essay on the Meaning of the Comic*. London: Wildside Press, 2008.

Billig, Michael. *Banal Nationalism*. London: Sage, 1995.

Brandom, Robert. *From Empiricism to Expressivism: Brandom Reads Sellars*. Cambridge, MA: Harvard University Press, 2015.

Buchanan, Ian. *Assemblage Theory and Method*. London: Bloomsbury, 2020.

Busch, Lawrence. *Knowledge for Sale: The Neoliberal Takeover of Higher Education*. Cambridge, MA: MIT Press, 2017.

Carlson, Chris, and Mark Leger, eds. *Bad Attitude: The Processed World Anthology*. London: Verso, 1990.

Carroll, Nöel, and Lester H. Hunt, eds. *Philosophy in The Twilight Zone*. Oxford: Blackwell, 2009.

Chalmers, David, ed. *Philosophy of Mind: Classical and Contemporary Readings*. Oxford: Oxford University Press, 2002.

Collini, Stefan. *Speaking of Universities*. London: Verso, 2017.

Crenshaw, Kimberlé, Neil Gotanda, Gary Peller, and Kendall Thomas, eds. *Critical Race Theory: The Key Writings that Formed the Movement*. London: The New Press, 1996.

Crenshaw, Kimberlé, Luke Charles Harris, Daniel Martinez HoSang, and George Lipsitz, eds. *Seeing Race Again: Countering Colorblindness Across the Disciples*. Oakland: University of California Press, 2019.

de Beauvoir, Simone. *The Ethics of Ambiguity*. New York: Philosophical Library, 1948.

Defino, Dean. *The HBO Effect*. London: Bloomsbury, 2014.

Deleuze, Gilles. *Difference and Repetition*. London: Athlone Press, 1995.

——. *The Logic of Sense*. New York: Columbia University Press, 1990.

——. 'Postscript on the Societies of Control.' *October* 59 (1992): 3–7.

Docherty, Thomas. *The New Treason of the Intellectuals: Can the University Survive?* Manchester: Manchester University Press, 2018.

Finlayson, Alan. 'Neoliberalism, the Alt-Right, and the Intellectual Dark Web.' *Theory, Culture, Society* 38, no. 6 (2021): 167–90.

Gadamer, Hans Georg. *Truth and Method*. London: Continuum, 2005.

Gibson, Chris, and Natasha Klocker. 'Academic Publishing as "Creative" Industry, and Recent Discourses of "Creative Economies": Some Critical Reflections'. *Area: Royal Geographical Society* 36, no. 4 (2004): 423–34.

Gilroy, Paul. *The Black Atlantic*. London: Verso, 1993.

——. *There Ain't No Black in the Union Jack*. London: Routledge, 1987.

Goffman, Ervin. *Behaviour in Public Places*. New York: The Free Press, 1963.

Habermas, Jürgen. *Knowledge and Human Interests*. London: Heinemann, 1981.

——. *Post-Metaphysical Thinking*. Cambridge: Polity Press, 1995.

——. *The Theory of Communicative Action*. Cambridge: Polity Press, 1986.

Hall, Stuart. *Selected Writings on Race and Difference*. Durham, NC: Duke University Press, 2021.

Husserl, Edmund. *The Crisis of European Sciences*. Evanston, IL: Northwestern University Press, 1970.

——. *Logical Investigations*. London: Routledge, 1973.

Jay, Martin. *The Dialectical Imagination: A History of the Frankfurt School*. Berkeley: University of California Press, 1973.

Kierkegaard, Søren. *Either/Or: A Crumb of Life*. London: Penguin, 2004.

——. *Repetition/Philosophical Crumbs*. Oxford: Oxford University Press, 2009.

Kuhn, Thomas. *The Structure of Scientific Revolutions*. Chicago: University of Chicago Press, 2012.

Lakatos, Imre. *The Methodology of Scientific Research Programmes: Philosophical Papers, Vol. 1*. Cambridge: Cambridge University Press, 1978.

Lakatos, Imre, and Alan Musgrave, eds. *Criticism and the Growth of Knowledge*. Cambridge: Cambridge University Press, 1970.

Leeming, David. *James Baldwin: A Biography*. New York: Skyhorse Publishing, 2015.

Levinas, Emanuel. *Totality and Infinity*. Ann Arbor: Duquesne University Press, 1984.

MacKenzie, Iain. *The Idea of Pure Critique*. London: Continuum, 2004.

Macpherson, C. B. *The Political Philosophy of Possessive Individualism: Hobbes to Locke*. Oxford: Oxford University Press, 1962.

McCollum, Victoria, and Giuliana Monteverde, eds. *HBO's Original Voices: Race, Gender, Sexuality, and Power*. London: Routledge, 2019.

McDowell, John. *Having a World in View: Essays on Kant, Hegel, and Sellars*. Cambridge, MA: Harvard University Press, 2013.

Mueller, Gavin. *Breaking Things at Work: The Luddites Were Right About Why You Hate Your Job*. London: Verso, 2021.

Murphy, Sinead. *Zombie University: Thinking Under Control*. London: Repeater Books, 2017.

Nagel, Tom. 'What Is It Like to Be a Bat?' *The Philosophical Review* 83, no. 4 (1974): 435–50.

Parker, Martin. *Against Management: Organization in the Age of Managerialism*. Cambridge: Polity, 2002.

——. 'Coda'. *Critical Sociology* 47, nos. 7/8 (2021): 1125.

——. 'The Critical Business School and the University: A Case Study of Resistance and Co-optation'. *Critical Sociology* 47, nos. 7/8 (2020): 1111–24.

——. *Shut Down the Business School*. London: Pluto Press, 2018.

Porter, Kerry-Ann, and Robert Porter. 'Habermas and the Pragmatics of Communication: A Deleuze-Guattarian Critique'. *Social Semiotics* 13, no. 2 (2003): 129–45.

Rawls, Anne. 'Harold Garfinkel, Ethnomethodology and Workplace Studies'. *Organization Studies* 29, no. 5 (2008): 701–32.

Reisch, George. *How the Cold War Transformed the Philosophy of Science: To the Icy Slopes of Logic*. Cambridge: Cambridge University Press, 2010.

Robertson, Craig. *The Filing Cabinet: A Vertical History of Information*. Minneapolis: University of Minnesota Press, 2021.

Rorty, Richard. *Achieving Our Country: Leftist Thought in Twentieth-Century America*. Cambridge, MA: Harvard University Press, 1999.

——. *Consequences of Pragmatism*. Minneapolis: University of Minnesota Press, 1982.

——. *Contingency, Irony, and Solidarity*. Cambridge: Cambridge University Press, 1989.

——. *Philosophy and the Mirror of Nature*. Princeton, NJ: Princeton University Press, 1979.

——. *Truth and Progress: Philosophical Papers III*. Cambridge: Cambridge University Press, 1998.

Rovere, Maxime. *How to Deal with Idiots (And Stop Being One Yourself)*. London: Profile Books, 2021.

Sellars, Wilfrid. 'Being and Being Known'. Proceedings of the American Catholic Philosophical Association 34 (1960): 28–49.

——. *Empiricism and the Philosophy of Mind*. Cambridge, MA: Harvard University Press, 1997.

——. 'Sensa or Sensings: Reflections on the Ontology of Perception,' *Philosophical Studies* (Essays in Honor of James Cornman) 41 (1982): 83–111.

Smyth, John. *The Toxic University: Zombie Leadership, Academic Rock Stars and Neo-liberal Ideology*. London: Palgrave-Macmillan, 2017.

Taylor, Charles. *The Ethics of Authenticity*. Cambridge, MA: Harvard University Press, 1991.

——. *Sources of the Self*. Cambridge, MA: Harvard University Press, 1992.

Thrift, Nigel. *Knowing Capitalism*. London: Sage, 2005.

Vaneigem, Raoul. *The Revolution of Everyday Life*. London: Rebel Press, 2006.

Wright, Steven. 'Beyond a Bad Attitude? Information Workers and Their Prospects through the Pages of *Processed World*'. *Journal of Information Ethics* 20, no. 2 (2011): 1–25.

Index

~

About the Authors

Robert Porter is research director in communication, media, and cultural studies at Ulster University, UK.

Kerry-Ann Porter is lecturer in the School of Communication and Media at Ulster University, UK.

Iain MacKenzie is reader in the Centre for Critical Thought at the School of Politics and International Relations at the University of Kent, UK.

Ingram Content Group UK Ltd.
Milton Keynes UK
UKHW011835230523
422239UK00002B/4